Notes to Grieving Friends

Notes to Grieving Friends

What to Say and Do When Their Loss Challenges Your Faith

Francis A. Martin

RESOURCE *Publications* • Eugene, Oregon

NOTES TO GRIEVING FRIENDS
What to Say and Do When Their Loss Challenges Your Faith

Copyright © 2019 Francis A. Martin. All rights reserved. Except for brief quotations in critical publications or reviews, no part of this book may be reproduced in any manner without prior written permission from the publisher. Write: Permissions, Wipf and Stock Publishers, 199 W. 8th Ave., Suite 3, Eugene, OR 97401.

Resource Publications
An Imprint of Wipf and Stock Publishers
199 W. 8th Ave., Suite 3
Eugene, OR 97401

www.wipfandstock.com

PAPERBACK ISBN: 978-1-7252-5529-6
HARDCOVER ISBN: 978-1-7252-5530-2
EBOOK ISBN: 978-1-7252-5531-9

© 2019 All information in this book is copyrighted by Francis A. Martin, Ph.D. It may not be copied or otherwise utilized without his written permission. To receive permission, Dr. Martin may be contacted by telephone, 615.585.4384, or by e-mail, Tncounselor@comcast.net.

All Scripture quotations, unless otherwise indicated, are taken from the Holy Bible, New International Version®, NIV®. Copyright ©1973, 1978, 1984, 2011 by Biblica, Inc.™ Used by permission of Zondervan. All rights reserved worldwide. www.zondervan.com The "NIV" and "New International Version" are trademarks registered in the United States Patent and Trademark Office by Biblica, Inc.™

Manufactured in the U.S.A.   11/26/19

This book is dedicated to those who grieve and to those who care for them. Please, take this book as an emphatic and heartfelt endorsement of your courage to love.

Contents

Acknowledgements | xi
Introduction | xiii
    Encouragement | xv

PART ONE: **Notes to Grieving Friends**

    What Can We Say? | 3
    Minutes to Hours | 4
    I Am Your Friend | 6
    Thank You | 7
    The Rose | 9
    A Picture | 10
    Love Now | 11
    You Matter To Me | 13
    Learn and Grow | 14
    We Grieve with You | 15
    Listen to the Rain | 16
    The Urgency to Care | 17
    A Blessing for You | 18
    Guide Us Home | 20
    A Gentle Surprise | 22
    What Will You Make | 23
    Seeds | 24
    Lines Come to Me | 25
    Welcome, Lord | 26
    Secrets | 28
    Good Morning | 29
    Think about Our Faces | 30
    My Mind Raced | 32
    The Shadow of the Cross | 34

CONTENTS

Life | 35
Love at a Distance | 36
Each Day | 37
Dawn | 38
Born Again | 40
Good-bye | 41
And Then God Comes | 43
For I Am Grieving | 44
The Now of Knowing Another | 46
Get Rest | 47
Your Strengths | 48
Source of Life | 49
We Are Quiet | 51
Alpha through Omega | 52
Danger | 53
Worn Boots | 54
Amateur | 55
The Gift of Memories | 56
Free | 58
We Wait | 59
A Simpler World | 61
My Experience of God | 62
This Day | 63
Count on Me | 65
Another Way | 66
Message Received | 68
Why Me? | 69
Believe in You? | 70
You Knew Us | 71
Savor the Pain? | 72
A Relationship | 73
Are You With Me? | 75

CONTENTS

Why Do You Cry, Lord? | 77
Intersect with Us | 78
Love That Lasts | 80
Lord of Risk | 81
Come, Now, Lord | 83
What Would I See? | 85
Living in Your Image | 87
We Know Our Need | 88
Making Sense of Love | 90
Joy, Bravery, and Love | 92
Epitaphs? | 93
We Look Up | 94
Needs Are Okay. Really. | 95
A Note to Jesus | 97
We Pray | 99
Truth Has a Heartbeat | 102
What More Could We Ask? | 103
The Game | 105
Hold You | 106
My Child, Your Child | 107
Welcome to a New Day | 108

PART TWO: **Useful Information about Helping Grieving Friends**

Basic Facts about Death, Loss, and Grief | 111
What to Say to Grieving Friends | 118
    What NOT to Say to Grieving Friends | 129
    A Final Word about What to Say | 131
What to Do for Them When They Grieve | 133

CONTENTS

PART THREE: **Grief and Faith**

Facing Grief with Faith | 139

    Understanding Grief | 140

    Is Grief Good? | 145

    Death, Grief, and the Christian Hope | 152

    A Blessing for You | 158

PART FOUR: **Grieving and Beyond: Encouraging Stories**

To Cope with Hope | 163

Ms. Nurse | 165

The Eternal Now | 169

More Than I Could Hope For | 172

The Last Word | 174

    The Moment | 174

    The Last Last Word | 175

Acknowledgements

The people closest to me when I have been grieving deserve the highest praise and acknowledgement. Through my demonstration of care for others who grieve and through this book, I hope that their sincere and immensely valuable support will be seen and felt, as a matter of their loving legacy.

My friend, Jan Turner, has provided superb editorial assistance. I am grateful for her professional and thoughtful engagement with the material in this book.

The people who received the notes in this book have challenged me, because they were grieving. They stood as a defiance of my ability to care for them during their most tender moments, sometimes overwhelming circumstances, and always pain. More than their challenge, though, they have allowed me to see life at its best, not so much because of their pain but because of their readiness to affirm life, despite their pain. They have been sources of inspiration and encouragement for me.

The thoughtful and responsive staff with Resource Publications/Wipf and Stock Publishers have been supportive, efficient, welcoming, professional, and very helpful, toward preparing this book for publication. They have my thanks.

Introduction

This book seeks to achieve something very simple. It is to provide "a voice" for times when we need to speak or write to a friend or relative who has lost someone to death. All of us who have been in the situation in which we needed to say or write something to a friend who is grieving know this need all too well.

While the title says that this book contains "notes for grieving friends," many of the notes will be useful in speaking to many different relationships. Surely, these include families. Also, they likely include employment relationships, church relationships, neighbors, and others. So, as you review the notes in this book, please consider how they may be used with a wide range of relationships. In fact, many of the notes were written for members of my extended family.

This book makes an important assumption: *Everyone grieves.*

While this may not be stated with great confidence, quite possibly our first experience with grief comes when we emerge into the world at birth and lose the secure comfort of our mother's womb. If this is not our first experience with grief, surely the first one comes soon after birth, when mother—usually, mother—leaves us in a dark room to sleep without her, again losing the secure comfort of her presence. Or, when a needed security blanket escapes our grasp, leaving us to mourn its loss.

Of course, as we "mature" through the first few years of life, we suffer many more losses. What happened to the pacifier to which we had grown so attached? Or, who took away the snuggly comfort of mom's arms when we suckled at her nurturing breasts? Or, the excitement of wrestling with daddy is "abruptly and crudely taken away," when bath time comes. Yes, from our earliest days, grief became a personal experience.

Naturally, for the sake of children everywhere, our hope is that loss and grief do not become the most visible features of their young lives, but that, instead, nurturing and enjoyable relationships have this place.

INTRODUCTION

Beyond the early years, though, when our understanding of loss takes incredibly larger meanings than misplaced toys or tired parents who cannot play as long as we wish, grief evolves into a heavier comprehension of the permanence and totality of our losses. Thus, if we live well, grief becomes something more than a reaction to loss. It stimulates us to protect ourselves from losing those closest to us, to value life in ways that children and youth generally do not comprehend.

Better understood, the anticipation of grieving as a fact of living tells us that living well and loving as thoroughly as we can qualify us to grieve well. Usually, we learn that to grieve is one thing, but to grieve alone is quite another. Grieving is much more likely to hold positive meaning and outcomes when it is shared with others.

As an expression of our need to share, *Notes to Grieving Friends* has emerged from serious attempts to "speak" to grieving friends and family. It is offered here as a useful resource. It is intended to help with sharing and with speaking to needs that are often difficult to address.

Part Two, *Useful Information about Helping Grieving Friends,* provides recommendations about very practical ways of helping grieving friends and family. The brief chapters in Part Two are these: Basic Facts about Death, Loss, and Grief, What to Say to Grieving Friends, and What to Do for Grieving Friends.

To be as useful as we can be, this book includes mostly notes to grieving friends. However, it includes more than the notes. Part Three provides a detailed statement about *Facing Grief with Faith*. This is intended to provide a way of thinking about grief from a Christian perspective and in a more expansive way than a one-page note to a grieving friend.

Part Four is *Beyond Loss and Grief*. It is a small selection of encouraging stories from grieving individuals that are intended to lift the spirit of those who read them. Each one comes from observing real experiences of individuals who have faced the stark realities of death, dying, grief, and making painful adjustments to some of life's most difficult changes. The encouraging stories include *To Cope with Hope, Ms. Nurse, The Eternal Now, Tears, and More Than I Could Hope For.*

Some of the encouraging stories reveal pain and understandable difficulty. So, please observe caution about reading these items, if you feel stressed or raw, with regard to your personal experience of grieving.

As you attempt to speak to those who have lost someone to death, God be with you. Remember that, as you help them, you may give attention to your needs, too.

Encouragement

When you or I meet a grieving friend or family member, the urgency of saying or doing something is clear. Unfortunately, what to say or do is not nearly as clear. So, to raise your level of helpfulness, I hope to provide some useful recommendations and encouragement. The point of providing recommendations is to encourage you to be as focused on the needs of those who are grieving as you can be. So, as you read the material in this book and consider how to help grieving persons about whom you care, here are some thoughts of encouragement.

One, please take any item here and adapt it to the needs of persons whom you want to help. While some of the items here may be useful just as they are, the odds are that most of them will need to be changed so that they "speak" to others in ways that you wish to speak. Because these notes come from a careful consideration of the needs of grieving individual about whom I care, I know that, for example, the note that I wrote to my uncle may not speak to your uncle. So, adapt the notes to fit the needs of the ones whom you love. This will likely benefit both of you.

Two, the hope that goes with each of the notes to a grieving friend is that it provides the friend with something that he/she needs. This hope rests on the idea that each note is suitable for the friend or relative to whom it was written. What this means is that it may not be suitable for another friend. Worse, if it is not suitable, it may be hurtful for the person to whom it is sent. Therefore, you are encouraged to read each note carefully before forwarding it to a grieving person.

Three, the titles for each of the notes merely identify the theme of the note. If you use a note to express your caring thoughts to a grieving friend, feel free to keep the title or to throw it away. The importance of the notes is that they help you to care for someone else in a way that expresses what you want to express and not so much to preserve what is written here.

Four, the notes to grieving friends appear on the pages here the way most of them were given to someone. Some have been slightly modified for inclusion here. All of them were changed so that they avoided the names of individuals to whom they were sent. Others were changed so that they excluded uniquely personal information that would likely have made them less useful for you. In addition, while most of the notes were sent, this book includes a few notes that were prepared for this book.

Five, the appearance of the notes to grieving friends is that they may have been written as "poetry." The appearance may be misleading. Much more than being poetic, the notes to grieving friends are intended only to be notes to friends or relatives, not expressions of art. For me, the notes are much more a matter of heart than of art.

Six, the notes to grieving friends may raise questions for you. They may raise questions about how grief works or how you may address the needs of your friend who is grieving. If you have questions about your grieving friend or your grief, please contact someone who can help.

Seven, because this book aims to help you to speak to those who grieve, feel free to say or write more or less than the notes in this book. If you wish to alter one of the notes or combine notes, please do this.

Grieving is painful. Grieving, though, is not the end of the story of life. Instead, although it is painful, it is a powerful confirmation of the importance of loving. In short, where there is no love, there is no loss and grief. In grieving, there is hope, just as there is hope in loving.

INTRODUCTION

In the story of life that rises above the limits of individual stories, such as yours and mine, God visited us in the person of Jesus and lost his life on our behalf. Surely, God grieved. So, despite our individual limits, grieving is another way of connecting us with God.

Janet P. Turner, Ph.D., Associate Professor with Lindsey Wilson College, reviewed and helped to edit this book. As a talented teacher, substantial and progressive scholar, a leader among professionals, and a good friend to me, I am indebted to her for her importance in improving this book.

Please allow a personal disclosure. Grief has come to me far more than I could ever want. I have been shaken and disturbed by some of my losses. My brother died as a very young man, shortly after he married and shared the expectation of having his first child. He died before his daughter was born. My sister lived much longer than my brother. When she died in 2012, I lost the only other member of my immediate family. Because she was one of my best friends, I have frequently felt her absence during the ensuing years. Clearly, I have not wanted grief. It hurts. This fact that has accompanied my losses, just as it has for almost everyone else. Inevitably, death will claim me, too, leaving others—I hope—to grieve my passing. Allowing for the inevitably of their pain and my obvious absence from their lives, I am truly grateful for the anticipation that they may feel pain, but not because I want them to feel the sting of grief. Much more than wanting them to grieve, I am immensely grateful for sharing life with them. Moreover, because I know them, I am confident that that the will grieve when I die, but I am more confident that they will gain strength from their grieving. They are hardy and full of life, after all. Just as I have gained strength from losing my brother, sister and others whom I love, those who succeed me in life will gain strength, too.

Yes, for me, grief usually comes as a threat, causing me to feel the void of life that may follow my loss. At least, anticipating grief provokes me to love more deeply and to decide more wisely how I love. To be more specific, I lack words to estimate the importance of the love with my wife, Martha. She and I share parenting of our daughter, Susan, and grandparenting of Emma and Megan. While I do not concentrate on or frequently focus on the likelihood of losing any of them or their loss of me, the fact of this possibility causes me to try to be as life-affirming with them as I possibly can. Indeed, my loving security with them allows me to expand the scope of life-affirming relationships with my friends. They are too many to name here, but I should acknowledge that as friends they have loved me when they didn't have to. Including the ones who have preceded me in death, how could I not be grateful for them?

PART ONE

NOTES TO GRIEVING FRIENDS

WHAT CAN WE SAY?

You have lost someone close to you. What can we say?

Well, we can say that your loss claims our attention, keeps us thinking about you with kindly thoughts, causes us to hurt for you, and holds steady our affection for you.

Is there more? Yes, there is more.

Now, comes rest. You and your mother may rest, now. You may renew your commitment to life, now. We will join you in this.

Is there more? Yes, there is more.

Remember, just as your mother knows love in death, love knew you before you were born.

And more? Yes.

Love knew you before you were born, knows you now, and will sustain you.

And more? Yes.

God knew and loved you before you were born, knows and loves you now, and will know and love you always.

MINUTES TO HOURS

Dear Friend,

You sat with Sarah, even when she could not know you were there. I saw how your moments of anguish about losing her turned minutes to hours. They were long hours for you.

During those long hours, your anguished face told a story. It was a story of wondering where God was. Where was God, when your need for God seemed most pressing and urgent? As one dad to another, I don't know where the love of God goes during such times.

With heart, though, I can tell you what I know. I have seen you care for Sarah during her long decline and at her death.

I can tell you that, crying with you, I know how very long your days with her have been and that for two years

> She slowly lost her ability to move
>
> She slowly lost her ability to swallow
>
> She slowly lost her ability to speak the thoughts that always came from her sparkling intellect

Your love for her weighed heavily on you and caused you to move slowly, too.

Does anyone know where the love of God goes, when your young daughter lays dying? Does anyone know where the love of God goes, when dying turns minutes to hours?

No. No one knows.

Surely, though, we know more about God's love than we don't know. Maybe, we can begin with the fact that my love for you lives as long as I live—and quite possibly longer.

And, your love for your daughter says that during her decline nothing else meant as much to you as her need for you. As dad to dad, you have given me lessons in loving that I cannot forget.

Does anyone know where the love of God goes? With all my heart, I would like to confirm that God's love

goes with you, even during those long, long minutes that seem like long, long hours.
    God be with you.

I AM YOUR FRIEND

If you need groceries,

I can make a run to the store.

If you need to cry,

I can offer a caring ear.

If you need to just visit,

I can be a good visitor.

If you need peace and quiet,

I can silently support you.

If you need a friendly presence,

I can be there with you.

I am your friend.

Grief cannot separate us.

I am your friend.

Grieving brings us together.

I am your friend.

As you hurt, so do I.

THANK YOU

Dear Lord,

May we give thanks? Thank you for the scribbles on paper from my four-year-old neighbor that she tells me is "I love you." Thank you for the seasoned and generous wisdom my old friend, John. Thank you for my friend, Ed, who called me when I was sick. Thank you for cell phones because they help me to keep my family safe. Thank you for music—rock 'n roll, jazz, classical, country, folk, reggae, Native American, and so much more. Thank you for nurses, hospitals, and physicians. Thank you for my high school yearbook with pictures that continue to embarrass. Thank you for blankets, especially on cool nights. Thank you for electricity and the hundreds of ways it makes my life better. Thank you for restful nights, when I have them. Thank you for books and the hard work from which their writers allow me to benefit. Thank you for convenient and clean rest rooms when I travel. Thank you for orange juice. Thank you for pets, even cats. Thank you for watches, especially my Mickey Mouse watch. Thank you for cardboard that sometimes makes life a lot easier. Thank you for political leaders with integrity and purpose. Thank you for e-mail that allows me to stay in touch with far-away friends. Thank you for grocery stores where I can get all the foods I want or need. Thank you for hangers that let me neatly keep my clothes in the closet. Thank you for football games, with a preference for the ones where my side wins, but thank you for all of them. Thank you for hot coffee on a cold morning. Thank you for airlines that help me to get to far-away places, even when they lose my luggage. Thank you for erasable markers and the white boards that make work more enjoyable and sometimes more effective. Thank you for marbles, along with other games, and the fun that comes from playing with them. Thank you for eyeglasses—enough said about that. Thank you for news programs that help me to know what's happening in my world. Thank you for razors, although my enthusiasm wanes as I shave each day. Thank you for sunshine and all other weather things that make life possible—rain, snow, floods, tornadoes, freezing and burning, although I have my preferences here, too. Thank you for numbers because they help me to make sense of things. Thank you for the sense of smell that lets me draw in the excitement of roses, gardenias, and other flowers. Thank you for air conditioning, for obvious reasons. Thank you for friendly and helpful clerks in the stores where I shop. Thank you for road signs that help me to get where I need to go. Thank you for conscience that also helps me to get where I need to go. Thank you for insect repellent that keeps me from being eaten during their very small meals. Thank you for love in which I feel more special that I could ever have imagined. Thank you for Your Loving Presence.

Today poses a challenge for giving thanks, because I have lost someone important to me. Still, Lord, You have blessed me. Thank you. Amen. Thank You. Amen.

THE ROSE

The Bud. Love begins somewhere. Often, it leaves us reeling from the feeling of excitement, surely knowing that the universe seems so small, without consideration of the special bond that you knew with your mother.

The Blossom. Love within your family grew, sometimes overflowing into others' lives, raising noisy laughter, and creating many memorable moments. Even when we were nuisances for her, your mother made us feel important.

The Beauty. Your mother's love pulled us into security, a quiet but constant knowing that she was committed to us so wholeheartedly that the security we felt causes us now to be wholeheartedly committed to you.

The Seed. We lived long enough with your mother's love to know that we learned love in such an important way that we could not and should not forget it. She taught us to say it again—I love you—and to make sure you know.

The Thorn. Love is interrupted today, but not broken. Love is confirmed as eternal, as we say good-bye to your mother. We may feel the loss, but she would want us to leave the cemetery and to love each other.

The Rose. Your mother's love hovers in my memory and fills me with joy, even while I grieve her passing. I feel the thorn of loss, but I savor the fragrance of her love and adore the beauty of the rose.

A PICTURE

You are a gift to me, a picture
of honesty and goodness, even
as grieving pulls you inward.
Your resourcefulness and courage
bring me thoughts of living well that
I had mostly forgotten.
You continue to teach me
about how not to be lonely,
although you have every right
not to share yourself with others.
You allow me not to be lonely.
You teach me what recovery
can look like, as you share
yourself with others.
I am grateful for your
honesty and courage,
in the face of your great loss.
You are a gift to me, a picture
of honesty and goodness, even
as grieving pulls you inward.
You teach me how to live
better than I would know
without you.
Thank you.

LOVE NOW

Love is never complete.
It's always in the process
of being made or unmade.
Just now, your love has been tested,
but it has not ended.
Do I see how you lack thoughts and,
maybe, feel words escaping from you,
as you try to think something or
find the words to express your loss?
None of your thoughts or words seem
to match the size of your grief.
Each thought or word that you search for
leaves you numb, compared with the
long and caring knowledge of your mother,
making tomorrow an unwanted void.
All of us know that this is a hard time for you
and your family, but we recognize how
our numbness and unwanted tomorrow
speak loudly about how deeply you care.
You are an example of loving.
My prayer is that the love that you
discovered and grew in the past
may be re-discovered and grown, again,
affirming the importance of your pain.
My prayer is that the love that you
felt from your mother may be felt,
discovered and grown again,

affirming the importance of your pain,
just as Jesus' anguished death
brought us closer to God's love.
For now, though, loving you in grief
is enough. Loving now is enough.
Be well. Love.

YOU MATTER TO ME

More than not knowing what to say to comfort you,

I care about you as you feel loss.

More than not knowing what to say to comfort you,

I want to share your grief.

More than not knowing what to say to comfort you,

I carry your pain within me.

More than not knowing what to say to comfort you,

I will comfort for you in any way that I can

because you matter to me.

Fold this page, carry it with you,

and open it when you need to know

that you matter to me—and to many others.

No matter how deeply you grieve,

we are with you.

And, no matter where you go,

I am with you

because you matter to me.

LEARN AND GROW

This is a prayer that I offer to God for you:

Lord,

Watch us learn and grow, for this is what you created us to do—learn and grow.

More than dying, you created us to learn and grow.
What shall we learn, Lord?
And, toward what shall we grow, knowing that death awaits us?

Lord, do we need to learn that when another human being suffers, we should suffer, too, and sacrifice to the extent necessary to eliminate their suffering? We remember that you instructed us to alleviate their suffering and, when we do this, we alleviate your suffering, too. Lord, help us to eliminate their suffering and yours. Is this the way we grow toward health, happiness, and life?

Lord, do we need to learn that through our readiness to give our lives for you we may find our lives in you? We remember your sickened sigh on the cross, "My God, My God, why have your abandoned me?" We remember that, in your teaching and in your dying, your discovery for us is that your readiness to give your life unified you with God.

Lord, watch us learn and grow, for this is what you created us to do—learn and grow.

More than being intimidated by dying, you created us to learn and grow.

As we face loss through death, now, we need to be reminded of your discovery that, through your dying, you unified yourself with God, as God.

What shall we learn, Lord? And, toward what shall we grow as we grieve? That we can be unified with You? To be unified with you through sacrifice and death?

Lead us, Lord, to learn and grow.

"For the Joy set before him, he endured the cross" (Heb 12:2, NIV).

Lead us, Lord to learn and grow.
Amen.

WE GRIEVE WITH YOU

"Invisible wounds are the hardest to heal. They usually depend on the love of others."[1]

As invisible as your grief may be, it is healed by the love given to you by your father. The flow of his love is now interrupted. This is the nature of loss—or so it seems—but it is not the nature of love and life. Life may be interrupted by loss, but, even in interruption, life is affirmed by enduring love—ours for one another and God's for all of us.

And, more than affirmed, loss gives us a chance to affirm you with love. As members of our family and as friends, we love you and grieve with you.

As a small way to affirm you, we have given a gift to _____ _____ _____ in honor of your father.

Our gift comes from our hearts because you matter to us. More than our small gift, though, God's "love endures forever" (Ps 136, NIV).

---

1. Said by a character during an episode of the television program, Call the Midwife, season 3 episode 7.

LISTEN TO THE RAIN

Listen to the rain.
It is a natural sound.
Your grief is natural, too.
And, just as the rain passes,
Your grief will pass, too.
As your grief passes,
I will help you to create
new memories, especially
new memories that help you
to celebrate the ones that
you have recently lost.
Listen to the rain.
It is natural.
It will pass.
And, so it is with grief.
My hope is that,
just as rain nourishes life,
your grief will nourish
your best memories and future.

THE URGENCY TO CARE

When I think of you,
the clutter clears,
    I think of you
    and have no need to schedule anything.
    I think of you
    and have no reason to plan anything.
    I think of you
    and feel no rush or urgency.
I think of you
and know only that I need to be available
for what you may need as you grieve.
The only need to schedule something
is to give attention to what you need.
The only need to plan something
is to plan to care for you.
The only urgency I feel is to
clear away any clutter that gets in the way
of attending to you.
Because you matter to me, the only urgency
is to care for you as well as I can.

A BLESSING FOR YOU

Give yourself credit for daring to live a life of service, to care for others,

and to let others care for you. All of this is important. But there is more.

May you gain spiritual health and keep it. As you do, praise God.

But there is more.

May you gain a clean conscience and keep it. As you do, thank God.

But there is more.

May you gain physical health and keep it. As you do, work for God.

But there is more.

May you gain emotional health and keep it. As you do, feel God.

But there is more.

May you forever keep family and friends. As you do, share God.

But there is more.

May you fulfill your interest in service and keep it active. As you do, serve God.

But there is more.

May you find joy in your life and keep it. As you do, sing to God.

But there is more.

May you feel peace of mind and keep it. As you do, live for God.

But there is more.

May you know the wisdom of living well and keep it. As you do, thank God.

But there is more.

May you acquire a serene and grateful heart and keep it. As you do, worship God.

But there is more.

May you find a place with the people of God and keep it. When you do, worship God. But there is more.

May you gain a clear sense of God's presence in your life and keep it. As you do, have faith in God. But there is more.

In God, there is always more. Be open to more. Claim it. Bless you.[2]

---

2. A version of this blessing appears in one of my earlier books: Francis A. Martin. *Full Life: A Workbook for Spiritual Recovery from Addictions.* Nashville, Tennessee: Green Hills Press, 2010.

GUIDE US HOME

This is a prayer that I offer to God for you:

Heavenly Soul of All Souls,

Let us **sing** a song of highest praise,

for you are the light that guides us home

where we may forever sing with magnificent voices,

the spirit that fills our hearts with hope,

and the majestic welcome that awaits us

when we arrive to be with you.

Let us **speak** with voices of impregnable sincerity,

for you are the promise of life fulfilled

without any reservation of giving yourself for us and to us,

the strength of presence that stays with us,

and the mercy that makes every morning a welcome one.

Let us **dance** with jubilant bodies and hearts,

for you are the life that fills all music

and the bodies who wish to express the life you have given us,

the soul that inspires the urge to sing and dance,

and the spirit of every sacred sound that gives meaning to all sound.

Let us **serve** with persistent dedication and joy,

for you are the one who served us with yourself,

when using your power for yourself would have impressed us,

the humility that makes masters of everyone else,

and the sweet gentleness that comes with redemptive power.

> Let us **love** in the manner that we wish to be loved,
>
> for you are the unlimited gift of love to us
>
> and the spirit of love that we take to everyone else,
>
> the caring presence that secures us in our love,
>
> and the transcendent being toward whom we move with all our being.

Now, in this life, we sing, speak, dance, serve, and love,

as we anticipate life forever with you,

when we can again sing, speak, dance, serve, and love.

We know that you watch us and smile. We hope that we are your creation

fulfilling itself. In this moment, let us be still and feel your presence.

In gratitude. Amen.

A GENTLE SURPRISE

And, then, a gentle surprise came to me.
    Butterfly One. Butterfly Two.
    Butterfly Three. Butterfly Four.
Butterflies. Four. Big ones.
More colors than I can count or describe.
More beauty than I can easily consume.
Butterflies. Four of them.
Seeing them means that, for a moment,
little else matters. They command attention
because they are there,
not because they want or need it.
Seeing you in your grief means that
little else matters. You command attention
because you are there,
whether you want or need it.
Just like the unexpected butterflies,
I can be a gentle surprise for you,
just as you have many times been one for me.
You are so very life affirming.
Even if you do not feel this,
you are life affirming and inspiring
even as you grieve—an example
of strength, honesty, and love.
Maybe, this is a gentle surprise for you.
Let's call it love.

WHAT WILL YOU MAKE?

I share with you the fact of losing someone.
I don't like losing. We share this.
For me, being without the one I loved
caused me to feel distant from others,
heavy and thick, not wanting to move.
For me, this is grief when it is most intense.
I am blessed by your friendship
and by knowing that your grief
is not a permanent condition.
You are free to make something of it.
What will you make?
How may I help you make it?

SEEDS

Seeds. Think about them. Seeds.
Apple. Acorn. Pumpkin. Each is really something.
Peach. Watermelon. Corn. From small things, big ones born.
Maple. Pecan. Lentil. I can hardly wait until
you stand straight, again, and honor your dad's passing.
I look forward to seeing your emerge,
as you grow from the seeds of life within you.
Just as your dad showed the rest of us how to live,
I can hardly wait to see your fertile mind
capture ideas that you share with the rest of us.
I can hardly wait to hear your laughter,
the roaring and inviting kind, just like your dad.
Grief will let you go.
You dad was so very good at planting
the seeds of life. I can hardly wait to see
what you become, as you grow with what
your dad gave you.
Your dad was so very good at planting
the seeds of life. And, so are you.
I am grateful for your dad.
And, I am grateful for you.

LINES COME TO ME

Lines come to me

to speak to you,

lines of hope,

swollen with feelings,

pressing and urgent.

Lines come to me

to speak to you to let you know

that you do not grieve alone.

Lines come to me

to speak to you,

lines that confirm

the importance of your friendship.

Lines come to me

to speak to you,

with the steadiness

and expectation of tomorrow's

sunrise and tomorrow's sunset,

certain and ever new,

just like our friendship.

Lines come to me

to speak to you

because you grieve

and because you are my friend.

I believe that God's desire

is that I should carry

the burden of grief with you.

This is the line that comes to me.

It is my line and my desire, too.

WELCOME, LORD

This is a prayer that I offer to God for you:

Dear Jesus,

May we have an honest picture of you as human-sized, just as we are human-sized?

Have we distorted our view of you as human-sized,

by building over-sized granite statues of you that make you non-human?

Have we distorted our view of your as human-sized,

by wearing Jesus tokens on gold chains around our wrists or necks?

Have we erased your human-sized presence among real human beings,

by seeing you as over-sized granite statues or little Jesus tokens that

that never have sore feet,

that never catch cold,

that never worry over their ailing parents,

that never dread going to work,

that never feel irritation because of inane television commercials,

that never consider the mystery of human reproduction,

that never say the right thing in the wrong way,

that never sweat in the scorching summer afternoon sun,

that never suffer with an aggravating splinter,

that never wake up with a stiff neck, and

that never gets stuck in traffic?

Have we distorted our view of you as human?

Have we made you so much bigger or so much smaller

than the cross-sized death you suffered?

Have we made you so much bigger or so much smaller

than the tomb-sized captivity from which you arose?

Granite doesn't weep. A gold cross doesn't weep.

We weep, now, with the passing of _____ _____.

Lord, we welcome you as human-sized, as a man

who suffered in ways that we suffer

so that we can welcome you as Lord-sized.

Welcome, Lord. Welcome! Amen.

SECRETS

Friendship has it secrets,
the personal knowledge
that binds us together
in ways that others may not know.
You hold as many secrets about me
as I do about you.
Even in your grief, seeing you
as vulnerable and unsure
about what your life may bring,
I feel safe with you.
You take me as I am, with every
"up" and every "down," and make
them into treasures to share and
some secrets to keep.
For me, this is the heart of friendship.
Just by being in my life,
you invite me to grow, to fulfill
the promises of which I am capable,
to care and to be honest.
And, now, even in your grief,
you make my life better.
You are my friend, secrets and all.
You are a wonderful gift.
I shall be there for you,
as best as I possibly can.
For me, this is the heart of friendship.

GOOD MORNING

If you stare at the crowded table,
full of your wife's presence,
looking at everything and seeing almost nothing,
you may be showing a sign of grief.
Grief requires attention, when other, normal things don't.
And, if you stare long enough,
the day passes from one to another
and the morning of another day comes.
No doubt, you feel your wife's absence
more than any of us could ever imagine.
The morning light of a new day is fresh,
bringing with it a sense of promise
that usually welcomes and awakens all of us to something new,
but not when we are grieving.
Grief holds us in a place of hurt,
making us neither present or absent, and
hides from us the things that we usually anticipate.
Because I care about you as you grieve, I wish that
I could offer a new day's light to you now and share it with you,
as if the morning and new-ness could keep us there, paying
no attention to time or grief, but grief requires attention.
My wish for you is that, as each new morning comes,
you may take assurance in knowing that your grieving
will end and that the loving memories you have
will stay with you, just as my friendship with stay with you.
Good morning, friend.

THINK ABOUT OUR FACES

This is a prayer that I offer to God for you:

Lord,
We are whole, now, but not perfect,
especially when we look at people we love
and people who need us and love us.
Today, we think about their faces and
about what we do to be sure that we see
their faces, again, knowing that there
are times when we will be away from them.
When we think about and see their faces,
the darkest day becomes bright,
because of their warmly provided love,
bringing assurance to us through smiles
and tight hugs, understanding looks,
whispers of special words of love, and
of course, meals taken together.
For them, Lord, we would give our lives,
to protect them and surely to save them
from any known threat or harm.
Lord, you must be surprised to know
that, maybe, sometimes we catch on
to what you have been trying to tell us:
You think about us and see our faces, too.
You think about us and see our faces,
while we grieve the loss of _____ _____.
You have loved us beyond possibilities
that exceed anything we could imagine.

You think about us and see our faces,
while we grieve the loss of _____ _____.
We thank you! Amen.

MY MIND RACED

Knowing that you have lost someone close to you,
my mind raced, with too many thoughts,
an avalanche of urgent thoughts
and not a useable idea anywhere,
in this moment of facing what happened.
Nothing to do, nothing at all,
except to face the simple facts.
    There you are.
    Grieving.
    Struck by loss.
    Here I am.
    Grieving.
    Struck by your pain.
When we meet the next time,
we will share our grieving, but
more than sharing grieving,
we will know that life is fuller,
kept in love, safe with interest,
and redeemed by loyalty.
We will not so much recover
from grief, but know that it is
one of the most common ties
that makes our relationship
a truly meaningful one.
So, yes, my mind raced, knowing
that you lost someone important to you,
wondering what to think and to say next,

but this is just a sign of how important
you are to me.
When we meet the next time,
we will not so much recover
from grief, but recognize that
it is another shared experience
that makes our friendship
a truly meaningful one.

THE SHADOW OF THE CROSS

This is a prayer that I offer to God for you:

Dear Lord,

Under the shadow of the cross, God of Eternity, those of us who are temporary need to know that all will be well for us some day. For this, we look to the cross.

We look to the cross for wisdom that helps us to rise above the self-protection that we know inevitably dies, along with everything else we have attempted to make eternal.

We look to the cross for wisdom that stretches us beyond the ordinary gift of understanding of which we are capable, knowing that the promise of your presence is more than we can comprehend now or accurately anticipate.

We look to the cross for ways to preserve life in the richness of the Grace in which you have allowed us to live and to find meaning and purpose in this, and to avoid merely casting ourselves to the winds of fate knowing that Grace explains much more than mere fate ever could.

Yes, we look to the cross so that we may know that when our days are gone, you may grant us the undeserved and welcomed gift of more days, even as we now offer you the life of _____ _____.

Lord, we look to the cross, as one of the sources of meaning and purpose that you have given us. Our prayer is that we may see the cross through fresh eyes, just as fresh as the blood you shed there and as fresh as the next breath we take, for they are the same.

Amen.

LIFE

Leaf. Rain. Light. Fire.
Fire. Leaf. Rain. Light.
Light. Fire. Leaf. Rain.
Rain. Light. Fire. Leaf.
    The order doesn't matter.
    It is. Life. Becoming.
    Life will create life.
Breath. Bones. Eyes. Sinew.
Sinew. Breath. Bones. Eyes.
Eyes. Sinew. Breath. Bones.
Bones. Eyes. Sinew. Breath.
    The order doesn't matter.
    It is. Life. Felt.
    Life is true to life.
Truth. Future. Beauty. Peace.
Future. Beauty. Peace. Truth.
Beauty. Peace. Truth. Future.
Peace. Truth. Future. Beauty.
    The order doesn't matter.
    Life matters and doesn't
    easily order itself.
Eternity. Life. Death. Love.
Love. Eternity. Life. Death.
Death. Love. Eternity. Life.
Life. Death. Love. Eternity.
The order matters.
Life matters. It is. Life.
It is life forever.

LOVE AT A DISTANCE

What do you expect, when the frost sits heavily on your feet because you have stood in place, moving only your eyes because you stand in the anguished cold of losing the love of your life?

As much as I care for you, your loss is so big that I can fill only a very small part of the large emptiness that you must feel.

Until the emptiness is filled, though, I will continue to give all I can so that you no longer feel the emptiness that you feel now.

Be assured of my love, while you grieve.

My love will come to you so long as you may need me.

This is not love at a distance; I will be as close as you need.

EACH DAY

This is a prayer that I offer to God for you:

Our Father in Heaven,

Each day is a trial. After we awake, feeling the fresh injury of grieving,

each day dares us to find meaning in it.

Today is a trial because we grieve,

a kind of pain that seems largely unfair.

You, Lord, found meaning in dying.

We struggle to find meaning in living.

You, Lord, inspired us by belonging to sufferers.

We struggle to exclude suffering from our relationships.

You, Lord, sacrificed yourself to death, in love.

We struggle to escape the pain of death, in love.

You, Lord, your suffering came from redemptive love.

We struggle to make our deep pain redemptive.

You, Lord, with kindly eyes looked after the worst of us.

We struggle with tear-filled eyes, while we grieve.

You, Lord, expose us to The Holy.

Allow us to struggle as we search for The Holy

in You and in ourselves, even as we grieve!

Let us make your struggles our own,

just as you made our struggles your own.

Amen.

DAWN

My grief closes in. I am alone.
Dusk. Trees. Gray. Nearly black.
Silhouettes. All is silhouettes.
No color, except gray, dark gray.
Feelings pull away from me,
as if a big vacuum pulls at
the basic meaning of my life.
I feel gray, like dusk.
This is the "low" of my grief,
but it is only one short scene
in a very long, epic movie.
Maybe, as you grieve, you feel
the way I felt when I grieved.
I guessed that those who loved me
could not understand my grief.
I hope that the way I felt
connects with you and your grief.
More than connecting with your grief,
though, I want to stay connected with you.
The darkest scene in this long movie
passes to another scene. As you live
today's scene and when you
get to the next scene, I'll be there.
After a while, I found that dusk
pointed me to the light of the next day
and hope. And, I found that the trees
that looked so dark—just silhouettes—

looked new, fresh and green.
The dark scene of my long movie,
in fact, moved to a brighter, newer scene—
a new day.
Your new day will come, too.
Dawn will be yours.
For now, though, as your grief closes in,
I will be as close as you need for me to be.

BORN AGAIN

When I grieved, you let me grieve.
You let me remove my mask and
expose raw feelings.
You saw the many secrets that
hide behind polite smiles
and casual best wishes.
You gave me permission to be myself,
with no hidden honesty or mystery,
no pressure to be something else,
other than stricken with grief.
My gratitude for your support
rises above my experience of grief.
Now that you are grieving,
you may be totally honest with me,
knowing that you are safe from
every demand to be something else.
When I grieved, I discovered
the importance of having you
in my life as one with whom
I could be totally myself.
Your love helped me to find
a new life and a new self,
as if I were born again.
I hope that I can help you
to grow beyond your grief
and discover a new life and new self,
as if you, too, are born again.
For me, this is what happens
in the love of friendship.

GOOD-BYE

She was saying good-bye
long before I could hear her.
She said, "I will miss you,"
with a strength of seriousness
that she had not shown before.
Why couldn't I hear her?
She was saying good-by
long before I could hear her.
She said, "You are beautiful,
as a husband and as a man,"
a very human affirmation.
Why couldn't I hear her?
She was saying good-bye
long before I could hear her.
She said, "No one is better
at taking care of the kids,
our beautiful kids, than you."
Why couldn't I hear her?
She was saying good-bye
long before I could hear her.
I needed to hear something else.
I needed her alive and well.
How could I hear what she said?
Why couldn't I hear her?
She was saying good-bye
long before I could hear her,
but now her voice comes to me.

In all the ways she said good-bye,
she needed me to hear her.
Now, I can hear her, clearly.
In her absence, I can hear
the passion in her voice, saying,
"I love life and I will miss it" and
"I love you and I will miss you."

AND THEN GOD COMES

Lord,

Grief had a grip on me.

I felt the twisted hurt of uncertainty,

knowing only that hurt and uncertainty

dominated my days.

Out of need to remember something

about the core of life, I remembered

cries of abandonment and separation:

> "My God, My God,
>
> Why have you forsaken me?"
>
> (Mat 27:46, NIV)

My twisted hurt of uncertainty

turned to awkward but growing

recognition: Pain connects us with God.

Grief comes.

And, then, God comes.

I hope that your pain connects you

with God.

FOR I AM GRIEVING

This is a prayer that I offer to God for you:

Dear Lord,

Your prayers for me make me uncomfortable, but I will try to hear them and to become the person that you expect of me.

Lord, speak to me:

The heart of the wise is in the house of mourning, but the heart of fools is in the house of pleasure. (Eccl 7:4, NIV)

When I was in distress, I sought the Lord; at night I stretched out untiring hands, and I would not be comforted. (Ps 77:2, NIV)

My comfort in my suffering is this: Your promise preserves my life. (Ps 119:50, NIV)

"Death has been swallowed up in victory. Where, O death, is your victory? Where, O death, is your sting?" (1 Cor 15:54-55, NIV)

He will wipe every tear from their eyes. There will be no more death or mourning or crying or pain, for the old order of things has passed away. (Rev 21:4, NIV)

[Jesus' Prayer for All Believers] My prayer is not for them alone. I pray also for those who will believe in me through their message, that all of them may be one, Father, just as you are in me and I am in you. May they also be in us so that the world may believe that you have sent me. I have given them the glory that you gave me, that they may be one as we are one—I in them and you in me—so that they may be brought to complete unity. Then the world will know that you sent me and have loved them even as you have loved me. (John 17:20-23, NIV)

I search the words of Jesus so that I may be able to speak to you as you grieve. Jesus' words, though, rise above my ability to speak to your grief just now. He said, "I have given them the glory that you gave me, that they may be one as we are one—I in them and you in me—so that they may be brought to complete unity. Then, the world will know that you sent me and have loved them even as you have loved me."

Lord God, be merciful to _____, for she is grieving.

Amen.

THE NOW OF KNOWING ANOTHER

Please, feel free to remove yourself
from the demand to be public with your grief.
Grief is never really public. It is always personal.
So, remove yourself from having to be public.
Let yourself find peace in being private, for
the vast expanse of public life can give you
very little just now. Keep your grief personal,
because grief is intensely personal.
And in keeping your grief personal and private,
surround yourself with those who love you.
Among those who love you, include God
when you can, because God gives worth to life,
including your life, as challenging as it is, now,
but God also gives meaning to the special one
whom you recently lost, your beloved father.
In God, you may find a transforming presence
and feel the peace and affirmation of life
that comes from God's eternal presence.
God gives meaning to life, including yours
and your father's.

GET REST

Nature seems to have endowed us with lessons
that are sometimes hard to follow.
One of them is that grieving takes a lot of energy.
Despite this, we push ourselves, as if we are not grieving.
Instead of this, would you take time to grieve and rest?
This isn't a demand. I can't give you a demand.
Instead, the idea that you may need to rest
is an invitation for you to accept, as needed.
Rest well, friend.
Think about rest. Get rest. Grieving asks this of you.
Be well, friend.
Listen to your worries, of course.
Listen to your loss and grief.
Work your way through your loss, not your memories,
for long after the pain is gone, the memories
will be with you as precious keepsakes for you.
And, remember to rest. The work of grief requires it.

YOUR STRENGTHS

I would never ask you to perform
and to look strong, while you grieve.
Grieving is too important to expect
performance and looking strong.
However, what I know to be true
is that grieving affirms your strength,
even when you may feel weak.
Knowing you as a person of strength
means that I can easily confirm that
you are a person who will endure grief
and become an even stronger person.

SOURCE OF LIFE

This is a prayer that I offer to God for you:

Holy Source of Life,

We acknowledge that you have gifted us with life, something that we could never have given ourselves. In response, we offer you a small sign, a small token, for your gift—our gratitude. We believe, though, that we should give much more than a small token or give you a small sign.

Holy Source of Life, just as you have given life to us, we aspire to give life to others. In this quiet moment of reflection, we begin with ourselves. We give life to ourselves by telling you that we are willing to sacrifice for those whom we love, but more importantly those whom you love, including those whom we have not yet had an opportunity to love. We are willing to give to others, even when it hurts, for we have concluded that our hurt does not compare with the hurt that you suffered for us and that our hurt redeems us and makes us whole. We wish to be whole and to live in the bright light of your grace.

Holy Source of Life, we promise to affirm life as we find it.

Show us those who are tormented by their children's self-destructive actions with drugs and violence and we will join them in their torment. Show us those who suffer aches and pains that come with disease and we will act as if the disease is ours. Show us those who see themselves as beautiful and we will love them as if they are real—in spirit, in looks, and in actions, making their lives ours. Show us those who see themselves as ugly and we will love them as if they are beautiful—in spirit, in looks, and in actions, making their lives ours. Show us those who are angry and we will accept them and attempt to meet their needs. Show us those who have substituted achievement for love and we will love them—wholeheartedly. Show us the children whose path has been darkened by absent and negligent parents and we will give them light. Show us those who are frustrated and fearful about their impending deaths and we will comfort them. Show us those whose souls have been hardened by their victimization and we will become a force of justice with them. Show us those who have withdrawn into desperate walls of loneliness and we will break through the barriers that keep them separate from a loving community and live with them. Show us those who are weakened by too much service to others for too long and we will serve with them, so long as service is needed.

Holy Source of Life, we aspire to be better than we are, because we are grateful for who we are—gifts. As gratitude, we aspire to be gifts to others. Amen.

WE ARE QUIET

We are quiet.

Nothing stirs. Stillness reigns. Time ceases.

We are quiet.

Listening comes easily. I hear only your hesitant breathing and your soft crying.

We are quiet.

Knowing you and wanting good things for you confirms this moment as sacred.

We are quiet.

Your grief—our grief—fills the moment with unforgettable togetherness.

We are quiet.

While still, we recognize that life could hardly be fuller than it is now.

We are quiet.

Why waste words in this moment? Words may report life; they don't make it.

This is our moment. This is our memory. In grief, we are making memories and

confirming love.

Life is this moment. Can you hear God calling?

ALPHA THROUGH OMEGA

This is a prayer that I offer to God for you:

Dear Lord of Time,

You are the Lord of Time, the beginning and end of all time, the Alpha and the Omega.

You are the arms that form the left and the right of our living, the Alpha and the Omega.

You are the welcoming presence at our birth and the welcoming presence at our death, the Alpha and the Omega.

You are the giver of life and the provider of life hereafter, the Alpha and the Omega.

You are the foundation of what we learn and the prize we seek, the Alpha and the Omega.

However, Lord, in between Alpha and Omega, we prefer to be in charge.

> During our "terrible twos," we are in charge.
>
> During invincible adolescence, we are in charge.
>
> As god-like moms and dads, we are in charge.
>
> As insured, money-saving, and retirement-planning, we are in charge.

Yes, Lord, from Alpha to Omega, we are in charge. We are in charge, except for the fact that we shall die. We are not in charge of dying or not. You are. Death tells us about our limits and your lack of limits.

As deeply set as our desire for being in charge may be, we must stop to acknowledge that you are in charge of death, but, moreover, you are in charge of life.

With you in charge, as the Alpha and Omega, our prayer is that you will also be everything in between—**Alpha through Omega**.

Lord, Alpha through Omega, be with us, as we grieve, for you are
> in charge of grieving, too.
> Amen.

DANGER

Grief feels dangerous, because we don't know
that we will recover life as we knew it.
Indeed, we cannot recover life as we knew it.
As odd as it may seem, life has a way of
discovering itself through grief.
After all, if we had not discovered life
before grief, we would not grieve.
Grief itself affirms life and how very much
we work to save it because
we love those who share life with us.
Grief feels dangerous because we don't know
That we will recover life as we knew it.
What we do know, though, is that we will
move into the future, one step at a time.
And, with each step, we will get ever closer
to knowing and feeling the promises of God.

WORN BOOTS

These boots are not in bad shape.
Old and worn, yes,
but not really in bad shape.
The deep cuts and ugly scrapes
bring to mind the events that happened
when they were recorded there.
One cut came when the ax slipped
And another from a sharp rock.
Life has its cuts and scrapes. None
is felt more deeply that the death
of someone we love.
My boots are no big deal, but
your loss is a very big deal.
Unlike worn boots, though, life
has a way of re-making itself.
Your life will re-make itself, too.
This is my hope and prayer for you.
The cuts and scrapes on old boots
really are no big deal. They come
with owning boots that are worn for work.
The cuts and scrapes of grief
are a very big deal and come
when we take the risk of loving,
for love and loss are hard work.

AMATEUR

When it comes to grieving the loss
of someone we love, all of us are amateurs.
This is the way it should be,
for we show much more interest in living life
than we show in mourning its loss.
Mourning is always amateurish.
Amateur comes from the Latin *amore*,
meaning "to love." For its earliest users,
it referred to those "who do something
just for the love of it."
For me, grieving is something we do,
just for the love of the person we lost.
If there is no love, there is no grief.
May you never become really good
at grieving, but, even in grieving,
continue to be really good at life and loving.
An amateur. As an amateur, may you
grieve well, knowing that you hurt
because you lost a loving relationship.
You are easy to believe, an honor to be with,
and a friend who invites discovery.
Grief and love are for amateurs.
I am ready to be an amateur with you.

THE GIFT OF MEMORIES
This is a prayer that I offer to God for you:

Dear Lord, Healer for us, grieving channels our attention and
brings into focus the memories that we cherish.
>   Birthday cakes that confirmed care for us
>   First-love kisses that confirmed care for us
>   Glimpses of the cross that confirmed care for us
>   Grampa's watch that confirms care for us

And so many more:
>   Mom and Dad's fiftieth anniversary dinner
>   The birth of our daughter, our first child
>   First moments at our wedding reception
>   The day we first felt your presence in our lives

Lord, will You accept our most loved memories
as small gifts for you? Along with _____ _____,
we give our gifts of memories to you,
for this precious person and these precious memories
define the importance of our lives in the most personal ways.
And, even while we grieve,
would you open our minds and hearts
to the possibility of affirming life
by creating new memories with those
whom we love and whom we serve?
Lord, would you take our grieving
and restore us with grit and an eye
toward creating new memories,
new blessings, and new confirmations of caring.
Restore us, Lord, with life-affirming gifts:

>Feeding hungry persons so that we feed you
>
>Comforting hurting persons so that we comfort you
>
>Accompanying lonely persons so that we accompany you
>
>Worshiping you so that we remember you.

We do these things in memory of you. Amen.

FREE

Free.

No tricks. No games. No pretense.

No charades. No threats. No coercion.

But free.

Free.

God makes every day a welcoming one,

surging with opportunities for you and me

to give to each other all of the best things

we have to give, because we are free to do so.

Free.

Today, the special gift that you give me

is your grief, for it tells me that you

may welcome me into your distress,

just as God welcomes you and me

into the warmth of a caring church.

Free. Gift of grief.

We are free to give and to receive

God's gifts, including each new day

and love, even when a loved one dies

and causes us to grieve.

Love and loss hold hands, while

grief and giving share an embrace.

Love and grief come best with freedom

among friends.

WE WAIT

This is a prayer that I offer to God for you:

Dear Lord,

We have places to go. At almost any hour of the day, we have places to go. We are very busy people. We hear our engines roar and our hearts race, as if getting there is a matter of life and death.

We have things to do. We never finish all that we have to do. No matter how much we do, we have more to do than we could ever complete. And, no matter how much more we wish to do, we do not wish to refuse another thing to do.

We have miles to cover. A hundred miles, a thousand miles, a million miles—we have more miles to cover than we can count. The places we go are important, but covering the miles is the really consuming thing.

We have people to see. We have many, many people to see. Neither their faces nor their souls matter, so long as we see them. We don't count them, but we need to know that we have seen them and that they have seen us. Why would we ever avoid being seen?

We have consuming pleasures in which to indulge. We have so many pleasures that deciding among them creates stress. We invite the stress, though, because it is a price we pay for pursuing as much pleasure as we can get.

Lord, we have places to go. We have things to do. We have miles to cover. We have people to see. We have pleasures to pursue.

Lord, can't you see how important we are? Maybe we need to explain this to you. In case you missed it, the point is that we are important. How could you miss this? Also, Lord, you need to keep us going. You can do this, can't you? After all, we are your chosen persons, aren't we? How could you deny us places, miles, things, people, and pleasures?

More than persuading you about our importance, we try hard to persuade ourselves. Lord, the places, miles, things, people, and pleasures seem so very empty.

They leave us hollow. Fill us, Lord. In this moment, we ask you to fill us, Lord. Fill us.

Fill us with a future that includes more compassion for others than places to go, more caring for family than miles to cover, more love for people than merely people to see, more presence for those who hurt than pleasures to pursue.

Fill us, Lord. And, Lord, we will be here with you, awaiting a future with you. Amen.

A SIMPLER WORLD

The secret of nature's world, a world in harmony with itself,

industrious robins,	scurrying squirrels,
rippling water,	swirling tornadoes,
hammering woodpeckers,	racing chipmunks,
wagging tails,	web-making spiders,
blowing breezes,	singing wrens,
communing ants,	lighting fireflies,
sparkling stars,	drifting clouds,
unfolding leaves,	ripening apples,
belching volcanoes,	warming sun,
falling snow,	budding black-eyed Susans,
nourishing rain,	renewing dawn.
rippling water	bluing sky
smiling faces	waving wheat

The secrets of nature's world, a world in harmony with itself.

Grief disturbs the harmony of nature, even if we know that it is natural.

Just as the disturbance is real, the harmony will return.

This is the eternal story of loving, losing, grieving, and restoring harmony.

God bless you.

MY EXPERIENCE OF GOD

My experience of God
is to the rest of my life
as the sun is to the earth.
God is the rest of my life.
God is the rest of my life,
including life beyond life.
For me, grieving hurts,
leaving me mostly confused.
Still, grief is transition, maybe,
to something much better
than I can now imagine.
May this be the same with you.

THIS DAY

This day appears to be one that came from of your highest hopes.

Today, you suffer the loss of someone important to you,

a loss that comes from living the high hopes

that the two of you shared for many years.

Without the high hopes of your relationship, you would not suffer.

You suffer the loss because the high hopes of your relationship

with _____ _____ are now interrupted.

Understanding the importance of connecting hope and loss

may cause confusion and pose challenges for us. It does for me.

The beauty of a shared relationship tells us something important

and calls us to see it.

    An orange peeled and shared.

    A ride to get the car repaired.

    Feeding birds together.

    Secrets shared and kept.

    Unique memories of love.

Life teases our senses with her tastes, sights, touches, and music,

usually because we share tastes, sights, and special moments

with someone who is important to us.

This day is a friend who invites us to live as fully as we can,

even as we grieve the loss of someone we love.

With death and loss staring us down and as painful

as this day is, the gifts that God has given us

have not gone away. Many of them are still there:

    Oranges.

    Rides.

    Birds.

    Secrets.

    Memories.

God provides for us because God loves us.

COUNT ON ME

When you are tired

after a heavy, long day of grieving,

count on me to let you rest.

This is what you have done for me.

When you are hurting,

feeling the grief of loss

of your irreplaceable love

and the snarling, growling loneliness

from the total absence

of someone intimately close to you,

count on me to hurt with you.

This is what you have done for me.

Just as you have taken care of me

when I grieved, I will care of you.

You can count on me.

ANOTHER WAY

You are a man of words. You speak more clearly and thoughtfully than most of us.

Along with others, I love your ideas—about almost everything—when you speak.

As much as you love ideas, they can get in the way—maybe guarding you from receiving love and support, now that you carry the pain of grieving.

I know. This describes me, too.

We are men of words. We cherish words, but they cannot cherish us in return.

We are sometimes left to care for each other without words. This is such a time.

Your loss transcends words.

Words seem to be a way of life for me. They are adventure, mystery, challenge, and much more. They are tools to use to repair all manner of others' brokenness.

They are friends, giving company when there is no other company to be found.

Words seem to be a way of life for me. They are a way of searching for ways

to confirm love and peace and justice. They express honesty, commitment, and

my personal way of knowing the truth.

Words seem to be a way of life for me, but never the only way. The more basic

way expresses more than words can show. The more basic way shows interest and

love—seeing you often while you adjust to your loss, hugging you, and centering

my attention on you and what I can do for you as you grieve, with or without words.

Words seem to be a way of life for me, but they cannot substitute for showing

love as well as I can. I will show love for you.

This is my commitment to you.

MESSAGE RECEIVED

This is a prayer that I offer to God for you:

Lord,

Your message has been received.

> Each of us is living proof of your enduring love for us.
>
> Sacrifice for others is always better than sacrifice for one's self.
>
> Each of us is your creation regardless of other markers of importance.
>
> You live with us in ways that may not always be clear to us.
>
> You provide for us, with food, flowers, friends, and family.
>
> You give us many truths and lessons so that we know how to live and die.
>
> You endow each of us with gifts that we should use on behalf of others.
>
> You equip us with the creative tension between faith and reason.
>
> You sacrifice for us and expect us to live sacrificially for you.

Lord, your message has been received.

And, we are grateful. Thank you.

Lord, your message has been received. Now, our prayer is that you will help us to hear your message, while we grieve the loss of someone we love.

Amen.

WHY ME?

It rains. I get wet. I complain. Why me? And then I see the kindly eyes of my friend whose son died in Iraq.

The rain doesn't seem so bad.

It gets cold. I get cold. I complain. Why me? And then I see the spirited enthusiasm of my friend who loves life. She lost her breasts because of cancer.

The cold doesn't seem so bad.

I get tired. I complain. Why me? And then I remember my father-in-law whose brave and loving encounter with death showed more courage that I can imagine for myself.

Tired doesn't seem so bad.

It thunders. I wake up. I grouse. Why me? And then I hear my granddaughter scream with delight when she gets new crayons.

The thunder doesn't seem so bad.

I sit in slow traffic. I complain. Why me? And then I meet my friend who needs a heart transplant moving slowly but with more determination than I can comprehend.

Slow traffic doesn't seem so bad.

I get bills in the mail. I worry about money. Why me? And then remember my mother who lived on a fraction of what I live on.

The bills don't seem so bad.

Even with reasons to complain, with you in my life, I am blessed. I am blessed with rain and cold and family and friends and money and much, much more. And each day, I am acutely aware of you as a blessing without whom I would feel bereft of life.

Although you may be rightly pre-occupied with your loss and grief, your importance to me will always be higher than you can imagine.

I am glad that you are in my life. I am grateful for you.

BELIEVE IN YOU?

Believe in you? Do I believe in you?

I believe in you

because you show diligence in nurturing your family.

I believe in you

because you drive with care that protects everyone.

I believe in you

because you give attention to your friends.

I believe in you

because you exercise and take care of yourself.

I believe in you

because you show unmerited confidence in me.

I believe in you

because you place honesty above recognition.

I believe in you

because you place family above all others.

I believe in you

because you believe in your friends, including me.

You make it easy to believe in you.

Remember these things, as you feel the pain of loss.

I believe in you.

YOU KNEW US

This is a prayer that I offer to God for you:

Dear Lord,

Before we were born, you knew us. Throughout our lives, you have known us. Beyond this life, you will know us, too, for you have made us and nurtured us for life, as living features of your creation.

In this moment, we ask for and expect little more than we have already received from you, for you have given us all we needed so far and have made our lives better than we could have made them alone.

In this moment, because this is a challenging time for us and those around us, we come with a need for assurance that you will be with us, just as you have been with us all along.

In this moment, attend to our needs and their needs, preserve us in your memory, and sustain us with your grace.

With its challenges, we are grateful for life and our relationship with you.

Amen.

SAVOR THE PAIN?

I hear you wonder about how you are grieving.

Do you savor the pain of grieving?

No, of course not. Still, because I have grieved, I understand how painful it is to let go. Letting go—giving up the pain and feeling good, again—seems too much like another loss, another way of believing that he did not matter, after all.

Do you savor the pain of grieving?

No, of course not. Still, holding memories of him as close to your heart as you can for as long as you can may feel like you want to savor the pain. Instead of savoring the pain, you are doing what all of us do. You want to preserve as much of the relationship as you can for as long as you can, knowing that the pain is a necessary companion to your best efforts to confirm the love you gave and received.

Do you savor the pain of grieving?

No! Instead of this, just like the rest of us, you wish with all your heart and soul to have the love you lost. The loss of love comes with great pain.

Ken Doka says, "The lessening of grief is not the end of memory or attachment; death does not end a relationship."[3] (1) Your memory of _____ without great pain will be yours. Your memories will bring you comfort and, probably, joy.

For now, the pain is real. The memories are real. Above all, the love—yours and his—is real, too.

---

3. Doka, Ken. "What Is Grief?"

A RELATIONSHIP

This is a prayer that I offer to God for you:

Dear God,

We really do not want to die. If we knew what to expect, we may be more willing to pass from this life to something else. For now, though, we anticipate something, without knowing what it may be. And, maybe, more important, we contemplate what it means to anticipate dying.

Why? Why do we contemplate what it means to anticipate dying? We contemplate because

> Your power **intimidates** us. We want power, but are stuck with the fact that we do not have enough of it to overcome death on our own.
>
> Your mystery **intrigues** us. We know how to solve mysteries, but we lack enough knowledge to open the mystery of what lies beyond death.
>
> Your grace **invites** us. We understand how to be gracious hosts and friends, but recognize that we often lack enough of it to achieve what we wish to achieve.
>
> Your sacrifices **challenge** us. When prefer not to know sacrifice, especially when sacrifice puts our lives at risk.
>
> Your promises **inspire** us. We keep our promises, but they are so much smaller than your promise of eternal life.
>
> Your endurance **frustrates** us. We know endurance and frustration, but only within the limits of getting what we want and when we want it.
>
> Your words **provoke** us. We love your words, but often hear them as provocations—words that invite us to be better than we believe we can be.

Your truth and love **expose** us. We believe in truth and love, but believe also that we must make a living, maintain a place to live, and keep up appearances.

Your presence **haunts** us. We need you and feel a little nervous about how much we need you.

Intimidation? Intrigue? Invitation? Challenge? Inspiration?

Frustration? Provocation? Comfort? Exposure? Haunting? Needs?

This sounds like a relationship to us. For this, Lord, we are grateful.

Thank you. Amen.

ARE YOU WITH ME?

This is a prayer that I offer to God for you:

Holy Presence,

Are you with us, Lord? How can we be sure that you are with us? After all, many things about you seem strange to us. Because of you, we work to make the strange-ness of grief more familiar, more sensible, than it is.

> We hear you are the Good Shepherd. Most of us have never met a shepherd.

> Many of us have never have never seen a sheep. Just like grieving, we need to make this strange Shepherd thing familiar. How do we do this?

> We hear that you changed water into wine. We have never seen such a thing. Somehow, just like grieving, we need to make this strange thing familiar.

> We hear that you fed five thousand people with just a few loaves and fishes.

> This is astonishing. Somehow, just like grieving, we need to make this strange thing familiar.

> We hear that you were a Holy Man who was mercilessly killed. What, if anything did, you do wrong? Somehow, just like grieving, we need to make this strange thing familiar.

> We hear that you came back to life a few days after you died. You came back to life? Somehow, just like grieving, we need to make this strange thing familiar.

> We hear that you loved your enemies. If you love them, they aren't enemies, are they? Somehow, just like grieving, we need to make this strange thing familiar.

> We hear that you give life. How do you do this? Somehow, just like grieving, we need to make this strange thing familiar.

Just like the sun and the air we breathe, we hear that you continue to be with us.

If this is true, somehow, just like grieving, we need to make this strange thing familiar.

Good Shepherd. Water into wine. Feeding five thousand people with a few loaves and fishes. Holy Man. Coming back to life. Loving your enemies. Giving life. God with us.

Somehow, just like grieving, we need to make these strange things familiar. Praying for your healing and Holy Presence, be with us, Lord. Amen.

WHY DO YOU CRY, LORD?

This is a prayer that I offer to God for you:

Sorrowful God, why do you cry?

Why do you cry? Sorrowful God, why do you cry?

Could it be that you cry because we cry?

Could it be that you cry because we are grieving?

Cry with us, Lord. Grieve with us, Lord.

Would it comfort you to know that we comfort one another, as if your sacrifice for us makes a difference to us?

> Would it comfort you to see us serving those who need us, just as you
>
> taught us?
>
> Would it comfort you to know that we seize every opportunity to make
>
> peace among ourselves?

Would it comfort you to see us giving generously of love and kindness to those who matter most to us?

Cry with us, Lord. Grieve with us, Lord. As you cry and grieve with us, what may we do to comfort you?

Amen.

INTERSECT WITH US

This is a prayer that I offer to God for you:

Spirit of the Living God,

Naked in spirit, here we are. Plain. Human. Needy.

Staring at the cross. Two simple lines that intersect. One up and down—vertical. The other from side to side—horizontal.

The cross. In neon, it brightly announces the location of the local rescue mission, telling the neediest among us where to go for food and shelter. We are not the neediest, today. So, this cross is not for us.

The cross. It poses in pure white snow, back-lighted by the moon and the golden glow from church windows beyond a serene, glowing lawn. We do not need a beautiful cross in a painting, today. So, this cross is not for us.

The cross. It stands above the town, holding the center of attention, as if it could add safety to those who live beneath it. As a steeple topper, it adds little safety—less than we need. So, this cross is not for us. .

The cross. It swings on petite chains of gold, glittering with pride from clean necks. As appealing jewelry and sometimes a reminder of meaning from long ago sacrifices, we need steadier reassurance than this. So, this cross is not for us.

The cross. It defines the church sanctuary windows, surrounding worshipers with the background scenery of glowing, colored glass. As a part of the scenery, we need something with more importance than this. So, this cross is not for us.

The cross. It speaks of divine sacrifice, a meaning-packed attempt to reach us when we suffer and to join us in suffering. As an ancient, present, and divine companion in our suffering, this is the cross we need. So, this is the cross for us.

Naked in spirit, here we are. Plain. Human. Needy. And, the Lord of the cross responds.

Lord of the Cross, although we may not see you or recognize you when we see you, be with us. Take our hands and lead us, again, to the cross. Open our eyes so that we may see the cross, again. Enter our hearts and minds so that we may follow You, the Lord of the Cross, and live our lives as children of the cross.

The cross. Two simple lines that intersect. Lord, we need this intersection. We need to be at the point of existence where you bring everything together—the vertical and the horizontal. Lord, we need you, the God of the cross. Intersect with us. Amen.

LOVE THAT LASTS

This is a prayer that I offer to God for you:

Dear Lord,

You loved us as infants. And now, as we have grown older, you continue to love us. We believe this. We are mystified by it, but believe it, anyway.

We lack sufficient wisdom and understanding to explain or understand who you are, how your love works, and why you love us. Despite this, we prefer to live as if we possess the certainty that allows us to live with hope, even if it is the hope that comes from our faith.

In the shadow of the cross, our prayer to you in this moment is that, just as you loved us before we were born, you will love us beyond the life we live at this time and will welcome us into a relationship with you that lasts forever.

Amen.

LORD OF RISK

This is a prayer that I offer to God for you:

Lord of Loving Constancy,

We know the weariness weary of running on the fuels of ambition, success, competition, marketing, achievement, winning, and beauty-pageant-like appeals. We like these things, but our problem is that these are the things that fuel most of us most of the time and that cause us perpetual discontent.

So, now in the midst of grieving,

> We succumb to raw ambition, as if we should achieve mastery of grief.
>
> We pursue successful grieving, as if we can graduate from it with honors.
>
> We compete in everything, as if grief can be beaten and we can be winners.
>
> We admire marketing, as if we can sell ourselves on overcoming grief.
>
> We love looking good, refusing to expose the unpleasant side of grieving.

Even when we grieve, our problem is that these are the things that sometimes fuel most of us and cause us confusion and discontent.

Our prayer is that you may be the Lord of Risk with us as we try to let go of our values that sometimes cause confusion and discontent for us, as we grieve. Will you share the risk with us, as we let go of ambition, success, competition, marketing, winning and looks as the values that shape almost everything we do?

Our prayer is that you may open our minds and hearts to adoration, praise, faith, ministry, worship and love so that we may grieve more honestly and authentically.

Our prayer is that we may see you as the **Lord of Sacrifice** with us as we let go of the values that serve us well, but that hurt us sometimes. Will you grieve with us? Our prayer is that you may be the **Lord of Living** so that what we do today matters more than looking too far ahead or too far behind. Will you be with us, now? Our prayer is that you may be the **Lord of Newness** so that everyday brings fresh, new challenges for us. Will you help us to feel hope in grief? Our prayer is that you may be the **Lord of Love** so that we may feel secure in our grief so that we live less with busyness and more with love. Will you love us, again, and expose us to the risk of hope that comes with love?

Lord, free us from the clouds of confused values and restore us with values that make our lives the lives that you have intended for us. Amen.

COME, NOW, LORD

This is a prayer that I offer to God for you:

Trusting God,

You gave us our lives to live in the hand of your favor,

> but we call on our hard work and our self-reliance.

You gave us an earth of plenty to sustain us,

> but we want more than you gave, shaming you as inadequate.

You gave us plenty for everyone, but we live

> as if your plenty should be reserved for some and not for others.

You gave us your love and a capacity to love,

> but we turn your love into our right to hate and to wage war.

You gave us the ability to dream and to know that life is a miracle,

> but we often choose to live dull lives, as if life may mean nothing.

You gave us more than we could ever hope for,

> but we despair, believing that we should be like God and less human.

Lord, you gave us yourself, as a sacrifice on our behalf, but we wonder whether you did enough. We choose to act on our own behalf, as if your sacrifice either was not enough or had not been made at all. Lord, plant in our souls the renewed capacity to believe in the miracle of your intervention on our behalf and in each one of us as miracle.

> Open our minds so that we may feel comfortable
>
> > with living in the hand of your favor.
>
> Open our wills so that we may sustain ourselves

with the good work of caring for your planet.

Open our compassion so that we may provide service

> for those who need what we have.

Open our hearts so that your love shows in our capacity to love

> so that we make peace—of mind and among all persons.

Open our spirits so that we may re-discover the ability to dream

> and to believe in the miracle of all life and act to sustain it.

Open our future so that we can hope beyond hope

> from the many gifts that are more than we could have hoped for.

Open our eyes, minds, hearts, and souls to the miracle

> of life with which you have blessed us, again and again.

Come, now, Lord, make us miracles, again. Renew our spirits. Fill us with consciousness of the fullness of life and the constancy of your presence. Come, now, Lord. Come, now, Lord, and remind us that you are here, that you are with us, and that you will never leave us. Amen.

WHAT WOULD I SEE?

Lord, can you tell me about who is there with you—in heaven?
Who is there with you? Who keeps you company?
Do you need anyone there with you?
If I were there whom would I see?
If I could see them, what would I see?
Would I see, maybe, Ronald Reagan or Lyndon Johnson?
What does someone like Reagan or Johnson do there with you?
Would I see a vagrant—a homeless man—and
maybe smell how bad his un-washed body smells?
Would I see my mother—a helpless, shriveled
old woman who had lost all mental capability
before she died. Or, would I see her as a vibrant,
lovely young woman?
Is she a mother there, with you?
Is she still my mom?
Would I see my sister—terrified but calm,
helpless in her hospital bed and then her coffin,
before she succumbed to COPD and cancer?
Or, would I feel her reassuring, sparkling
blue eyes letting me know that I am still loved
by my big sister? What stories would she tell about you?
Would I see their disease-ravaged bodies?
Or, would I see a vagrant, my mother, and my sister
bathed in brilliant white rose petals, smiling as if
their joy had only begun and would never end?
Who is there with you? And, where are you?
And, why would I want to see any of this?

May I have some answers?

Do you have any answers, Lord?

Friend, sharing your questions comes as inspiration for me.

Thank you.

LIVING IN YOUR IMAGE

This is a prayer that I offer to God for you:

Dear Lord,

This stretches our usual thinking about loss and grief, but we are grateful for it because it connects us with you and your grief.

We understand that we are made in your image and that, because of this, something sacred may be seen in us, even if we understand, too, that we may be a blurred reflection of You.

So, in this moment of serious thought, we pray that your image of you may be seen, by the way we are and by what we do.

We pray that we may show a picture of piety, a sign of integrating our image with yours and become in appearance and action more like You.

Make us the unmistakable sign of your work among us and the living proof of your presence.

We pray that every individual interaction, as fragmented and incoherent as it may appear, will conclude with grace and hope, in the same way that your example may have been fragmented and incoherent, but ended with beaming grace and joyful hope.

So, our prayer is that you will accept our human and obviously limited, but—as sincere and real as we can be—gratitude. For the mere possibility and maybe the real potential of living in your image, we are grateful.

This stretches our usual thinking about loss and grief, but we are grateful for it because it connects us with you and your grief.

Amen.

WE KNOW OUR NEED

This is a prayer that I offer to God for you:

Dear Heavenly Guide,

We know right from wrong. Really, we know. We know.

We understand the difference between right and wrong.

Despite knowing right from wrong, we sometimes

    over-feast with holiday meals

    neglect exercising our bodies

    smoke or chew tobacco

    keep harmful secrets

    drive in insane ways

    drink to excess

    pretend to know more than you

    bare our claws in anger

    let reason subdue our faith

    worry too much about tomorrow

    get frustrated with rain or snow

    neglect needy persons

    forget to say, "I love you."

    withhold speaking the truth

    neglect a beautiful sunset

Lord, you get the idea. We know. We know right from wrong.

Just now, Lord, we acknowledge who we are.

Because of our universal human barrenness,

our ordinary and undeniable weakness,

we need you to be The Heavenly Guide

to whom we give as much attention

as our human limitations allow.

We know our need for You, including
our need for help with life, death and grieving.
This, we know. We know.
Thank you. Amen.

MAKING SENSE OF LOVE

This is a prayer that I offer to God for you:

Dear Lord,

How do we make sense of your love for us?

You love us, when you are not obligated

to love us, so much more than we deserve,

except by your decision to love us.

And, now, Lord,

our prayer is that you may accept

our love for you,

because we have decided to love you.

Today, we give our grief to you,

as an expression of our love for you,

in this raw and very personal way.

Within the bond we have with you,

we offer gestures of love for you:

> We offer losing,
>
> > but with the expectation of a return of hopefulness.
>
> We offer aching,
>
> > but with the need for a return of Holy affection.
>
> We offer crying,
>
> > but with the honest desire for genuine bravery.
>
> We offer confusion,
>
> > but with the sincerity that invites your caring.

With little more to offer,

remembering your transcendent love

> praying with barren, open souls
>
> seeking service, imitating you

loving others, as openly as you
love us and with as much risk.
In love. Amen.

JOY, BRAVERY, AND LOVE

This is a prayer that I offer to God for you:

Lord,
Yes, we are acquainted with emptiness
and the echoes in our hearts that remind us
of our capacity for loneliness. And,
we are acquainted with overflowing **joy**
and the explosive importance of letting
everyone else in the world know
how important we are because of You.
Yes, we are acquainted with **bravery**
that we tuck neatly in places where
bravery lacks comfort and honesty. And,
we are acquainted with personal renewal
that takes us to important places where
others need to see our lives as samples
of your efforts toward exposing Truth.
Yes, Lord, we are acquainted with **love**
and our sometimes inclination to hum
through moments when we should sing
love loudly—really loudly! And, we
are acquainted with the outrageous yell
of love letting go in the life-giving gamble
that love always works hard, naturally!
As demanding and compelling as grief is,
we are acquainted with joy, bravery and
love within the pain of grieving
because we are acquainted with You.
With joy, bravery and love,
Thank you. Amen.

EPITAPHS?

This is a prayer that I offer to God for you:

Gracious Lord,
We have seen how the seasoned craftsman
takes wood that is, well, formless, if not ugly
and makes a beautiful, useful table from it.
We marvel at how he twists his strong hands
with tools that seem to perform miracles, as the
formless wood takes the form of a table.
The pace of our understanding confines us,
leaving us lagging behind the craftsman, as he
builds his epitaph, bequeathing himself.
Lord, we stay tuned to your intentions
for us, as You shape our formless selves and
perform miracles with your strong hands.
Our pace of understanding lags behind
Your gracious, divine craftsmanship
that transforms us into your living epitaph,
In our grief, may we become true examples
of genuine understanding and real faith and,
like the craftsman's table, living epitaphs.
Amen.

WE LOOK UP

The man slumped.

His heavy shoulders were too much.

He looked down and

never looked up again.

The man felt despair.

He knew that he was going to die.

He looked down and

never looked up again.

The man barely breathed.

His injuries compromised his life.

He looked down and

never looked up again.

The man cried in anguish.

His pain saturated his bloody body.

He looked down and

never looked up again.

The man slumped.

His weakness told of his dying.

He looked down and

never looked up again.

The man died alone.

He died as a despised criminal.

He looked down and

never looked up again.

The Man looked down

on the dark day of his death and

we have looked up to him

from the day he arose.

NEEDS ARE OKAY. REALLY.

Dear Friend,

You know how easily we can speak in quips. You and I can quickly crack the moment with just the right quip. It comes easily.

> What goes around comes around.
>
> The bigger they are the harder they fall.
>
> Better to have loved and lost than never to have loved at all.
>
> Only the lead dog has a change of view.
>
> There is no "I" in "team."
>
> Any day above dirt is a good one.
>
> If you want a job done right, do it yourself.
>
> Do unto others as you would want them to do unto you.
>
> There's no such thing as an unimportant life.
>
> All is fair in love and war.
>
> Remember to never mix politics and religion.
>
> Nothing risked, nothing gained.
>
> Take care of number one. No one else will.
>
> Live may not be great, but it sure beats the alternative
>
> Act today as you want to remember yourself tomorrow.

After all the quips, what do we have to say? In times like this, what do we have to say? What happens when we speak openly from our hearts? What do we say? Can we open our hearts to truth and speak?

You grieve because you lost _____.

Okay. Let's silence ourselves for a moment. Let's acknowledge that the quips—as clever as they are—may distract us from openly loving each other. With no quips,

I need you. And, needs are okay. Really. Your needs are okay, too.

We may not be much, but God loves us, anyway. No quips. No clever attempts to be wise. God loves us, anyway. And, our need for God's love is okay. Really.

A NOTE TO JESUS

I am flesh.
> You are soul.

I am part.
> You are whole.

I am blind.
> You are sight.

I am dark.
> You are light.

I am war.
> You are peace.

I am want.
> You are feast.

I am doubt.
> You are truth.

I am death.
> You are youth.

I am dull.
> You are sharp.

I am rock.
> You are harp.

I am seek.
> You are find.

I am thought.
> You are mind.

I am print.
> You are page.

I am dull.

> You are sage.

I am sad.

> You are zeal.

I am grief.

> You are heal.

I am man.

> You are God. Amen.

WE PRAY

Lord,

We stand at the gates of hope, with the monument to hope, our church, towering over us.

We hear the beat of expectant hearts, knowing the deep kindness of ordinary saints.

We cheerfully drift toward full-voiced mouths of the richest lyrical and gritty love.

We pay the toll on the road to honest service for those who cannot serve us.

We fight all and every attempt to abolish hope, knowing that you died for ours.

We touch the meaning of deity, as we feel the cool rain on our upward faces.

We weep when we cannot loudly scream the joy that fills us with knowledge of you.

We carry the debt of love that we re-pay to those who cannot pay us anything.

We remember that you teased us with the mystery of visiting with us a while back.

We grasp the mystery of your presence, as surely as we breath air we cannot see.

We stand behind the shield of the crackling, banging tragedy of your sacrifice for us.

We sing about the blessed storm of life-sustaining gifts that you have left for us,

but in sounds that arise in the quiet and solemn brightness exclusive to faith in you.

We speak in tender voices and caring words that drive us toward one another in love.

We reflect on the reality of serenity that comes from the reality of your love for us.

We suppress the confident shouts of needing better lives for those who search for you, but have not yet opened their hearts to you and found you.

We search to discover the warmth of child-like dreams of enjoying to your perfect will.

We probe every dark inch of our souls, affirming the need to pry them open for you.

We know the right way to live and solicit your energizing presence to enable us to do it.

We wait for your shepherding presence, while we work dedicatedly to shepherd others.

We watch with wide-open eyes the playful joy of children and seek to imitate them.

We burn with passion for life—all lives—including our own and the life you offer us.

We whisper quiet assurance of unremitting presence and comfort for those who suffer the impending loss of their lives and the loving persons who will lose them.

We sleep and rest to restore ourselves so that we may serve you energetically.

We forget the injuries and insults that come to us when we faithfully serve you.

We burst with unexpected pleasure, when we help to cancel pain in others.

We separate ourselves from oppression, bigotry, and aggression, on your behalf.

We block lies, impulses to skew truth, and urges to harm, because of you.

We welcome opportunities for praise of your astonishing creation, including us.

We condone peace and seek to establish and sustain peace, just as you gave us peace.

We long for reasons that confirm faith and for faith that confirms reasons.

We clinch our fists, in defiance of indifference, ignorance, and greed, for you.

We pray. We pray, with gratitude. Thank you for your irreplaceable gifts for us.

Lord, we feel overwhelming honor to have been made in your image. Thank you.

Amen.

TRUTH HAS A HEARTBEAT

This is a prayer that I offer to God for you:

Lord,

We know the Truth. You are the Truth. We love the Truth.
We seek to live in the Truth, with honest truth-in-action commitment.
We recognize the necessary limits of life that urge us to believe in you.
We expect to express your loving spirit toward everyone we know.

And, then, we see ourselves. We know ourselves. We are the truth.
And, we feel in the depths of our best knowing that the half-truths
by which we live provide us the luxury of the strongest prisons,
prompting us to bow to the self-satisfied whispers in our minds.

Enter our lives, our hearts, our decisions, our planning, our owning,
so that we may know The Truth. Enter our lives so that we know
The Truth, as surely as we know the reassurance of heartbeats,
remembering that you relinquished your human heartbeat for us.

Lord, as slowly as we age, we learn that pain is a great teacher,
inviting us to recognize the limits of life that urge us to believe in you
and to find security in the imminence of your loving presence and
know The Truth as surely as we know the challenge of dying.

Amen.

WHAT MORE COULD WE ASK?

Your questions speak to me.

We ask questions, don't we? We have hundreds of questions or, maybe, thousands. After losing someone close to us, we have questions, if nothing else, because we are left to wonder, "What next?"

Mostly, your questions and mine tell us that we don't understand nearly as much about our lives and the way life works as we should. We need to challenge the idea that we can easily find comfort in grieving. Sometimes, we can't. It hurts too much.

Like you, I feel the questions. For me, grieving is not so much about raising questions for which I expect immediate answers. It is much more about feeling the loss. How do I fit the pieces of my life together, without her? How do I make sense of my relationships, now that she is no longer one of my relationships? How long is it until I no longer hold images of her decaying and fragile body? Again, for me these are more things that I feel than I think about.

Questions are real. They press for movement toward answers, but answers take a while.

I feel the questions. And, then, I see the cross. The cross can remind me of sacrifice that is larger than I have given, more than I am capable of giving. I see suffering that is more severe than I have carried, more than my strongest moments could tolerate. I see loss that is greater than I have sustained, loss that would probably kill me. And, I see love that is much more than I have done or imagined, more than enough to test my imagination about what love can be.

I see the cross and His sacrifice, suffering, loss, and love. And, I still feel the questions. This is some of the meaning of loss and life. For me, meaning is never static. It is always evolving.

You and I feel the questions. Then, we see the cross. And, in seeing the cross, we get glimpses of the concern that God has for us, including concern for our questions. Our questions are real, just as His suffering on our behalf and the love that showed itself in suffering are real, too. We see the cross and, possibly, how insignificant our questions may be.

My prayer for you now is that you may feel the significance of your questions, along with feeling the significance of God's sacrifice, suffering, loss, and love for you and your questions.

And, when we feel our questions—real and pressing—and see what God did, I wonder, "What more could we ask?"

THE GAME

Underneath the guessing game grow the thorns of doubts that hurt when I touch the memories of loving you.

The game.

It touches me.

It leaves me imagining forever as a peaceful retreat from the pain of losing you.

It forges big ideas about how pleasantly I may be able to terminate my torment—my grief and loneliness.

It surrounds me with poetic pictures of bad things that persist in causing me to wish for a simple end to my long and dragging depression.

It purveys the promising pause of eternal poise, bringing an end to the serious pain.

It invites me to join you in your passage from this life to something else.

It buckles my knees from the burden of hopelessness.

And I cry.

Privately, of course.

The feeling of loss turns my head to memories of times when I knew your presence, when I held you and you held me, when you revealed your secrets to me and I revealed mine to you, when we kissed, when we talked until we fell asleep, remembering where the conversation was but not remembering who said something last.

Loss has a way of working me into the past I shared with you.

And then I hear your voice echoing in my head:

"Get on with your life, you darn fool! You're not dead, yet."

The memory of your love helps me to discover life as new.

HOLD YOU

Hold you. Maybe, that's all I can do.
I can hold you. I can't say something
that will take away the pain of losing
someone close to you, but I can
hold you.
I can't say much, but can hold you,
with the hope that you can feel
how much you matter to me and
how much I want you to feel
the durability of my love for you.

MY CHILD, YOUR CHILD

This is a prayer that I offer to God for you:

Dear God,

Listen. Listen to my heartbeat. Listen to my heartbeat, as I listen to the heartbeat of my baby girl. In her heartbeat, I can hear you calling me. Life, my life, is renewed through her. She cries and touches my soul with music, the sounds of a million, welcoming choirs with the sweetest voices, quieting the world around me. She breathes softly and, in her unaware innocence, warms our shared space, as if the sun stopped to bow before her and warm us for a while. She gently sleeps in my arms and awakens me to your presence—enveloping, quiet, holy, and powerful.

Enveloping, quiet, holy, and powerful: And I remember,

Do not be anxious about anything, but in every situation, by prayer and petition, with thanksgiving, present your requests to God. And the peace of God, which transcends all understanding, will guard your hearts and your minds in Christ Jesus. (Phil 4:6-7, NIV)

In this quiet time, I can hear you calling. "Be natural, like a young bird flying. Let go of pretense, like a stream flowing over your bare feet. Let your brokenness become whole, secure in the future that your baby daughter promises. Welcome love, just as I welcome you with mine. And, walk with hope into your future, knowing that you are connected with your daughter and with my love."

Dear God, my child touches my soul and brings me to you.

God has a way of renewing us, including you.
Amen.

WELCOME TO A NEW DAY

Our days do not feel new when we grieve.
Instead, they hang heavily on us.
We don't sleep as well as we used to.
We long for our day to be over, only
to find that it feels like it goes on
forever, even when we know it's over.
No matter now long your day seems
to you, would you remember that
God is a friendly, loving presence
who welcomes you to every day
as new and full of possibilities.
If today is not your new day,
please hold the idea that it will come.
And, when your new day comes,
I will be there to say to you,
"Welcome to your new day."

PART TWO
USEFUL INFORMATION ABOUT HELPING GRIEVING FRIENDS

Basic Facts about Death, Loss, and Grief

The collection of information in this chapter may surprise no one. It is intended only to bring a small measure of objectivity to a common life experience that is not objective. Grieving is almost always a deeply personal experience. It is not objective. The importance of objectivity is that it may help those among us who want to assist grieving persons. This is the importance of the collection of information in this chapter.

The information in this chapter may help us to be sensitive to many kinds of loss. For example, the miscarriage of a pregnancy is a significant loss. Likewise, moving from a familiar community where relationships are established and secure to a community where few, if any, important relationships exist, can be an important loss, too. Sometimes, a divorce that follows from a seriously troubled marriage causes grief. The cause of grief may take many different forms.

Did you know? Beyond our earliest years, we suffer loss and, because of this, grieve. This is to say that grieving is unavoidable. The information below illustrates both the inevitability of grief and that is affects almost everyone.

Approximately, three million (3,000,000) Americans die each year.[1]

According to the Centers for Disease Control and Prevention, "Suicide is a public health problem that takes a life in the United States about every 12 minutes. Suicide rates have increased by nearly 30% from 1999 to 2016, and effective prevention programs and policies are needed to stop this upward trend."[2] In recent years, approximately forty-five thousand (45,000) individuals took their own lives in the United States.[3] Obviously, the loss of an individual

1. "Death and Mortality." Centers for Disease Control and Prevention.

2. "Preventing Suicide in the United States." Centers for Disease Control and Prevention

3. "Preventing Suicide in the United States." Centers for Disease Control

to suicide has a direct impact on the lives of a much larger number of those who survive the loss.

Approximately, one third of deaths occur from natural causes, relatively late in life and that a very high percentage of deaths come from natural causes.[4]

Death is anticipated for approximately two thirds of those who die each year, usually from various illnesses, such as cancer, heart disease, and diabetes. However, while death is anticipated, it comes at an earlier age than anticipated because of these diseases.[5]

By a wide margin, accidents are the leading cause of death for children under age eighteen. They are also the cause of many disabling injuries, creating loss of mobility, fine motor skills, and cognitive functions.[6] "Age is the predominant risk factor for death due to unintentional injury. The very young, particularly males, are prone to unintentional injuries because their lack of knowledge and experience leads them to engage in high-risk behavior"[7]

Currently, approximately five hundred thousand (500,000) children live in foster care. The importance of this is that these children have suffered huge personal losses and, sadly, various forms of victimization in a large percentage of their lives. For these children, grieving and trauma are common features of their experience.[8]

Life-long grief sometimes accompanies individuals whose marriages end in divorce. According to *Grief Speaks*, approximately forty-three percent of marriages end in divorce.[9]

---

and Prevention
    4. Untitled. Centers for Disease Control and Prevention.
    5. Untitled. Centers for Disease Control and Prevention.
    6. Untitled. Centers for Disease Control and Prevention.
    7. Untitled. Centers for Disease Control and Prevention.
    8. Child Welfare Information Gateway. (2019). *Foster care statistics 2017*.
    9. "Grief Speaks." Grief Speaks.

Divorce Statistics

- 68.7% of American youth are living in non-traditional families. This is 7 out of 10
- 23.3% living with biological mother
- 4.4% living with biological father
- 1% Foster Families
- 3.7% living with non-relatives
- 6.3% living with grandparents
- 30% living in Step-families

Grief occurs on a large scale, in response to overwhelming natural events, such as a hurricane. In 2017, Hurricane Harvey caused one hundred twenty-five billion dollars in damage. The monetary loses overwhelmed countless individuals and families. More than the monetary loses, though, Hurricane Harvey killed eighty-eight individuals.[10]

"In 2018, about 11.69 million widows were living in the United States, whereas the number of widowers was at about 3.41 million."[11] Combined, the number of widows and widowers is more than fifteen million individuals. Needless to say, no matter what the causes of the deaths that led to their current status, these individuals have suffered considerable loss.

Between 35% and 48% of college students have lost a family member or close friend within the last two years. Between 22% and 30% of college students have lost a family member or close friend within the last year (Balk, 1997; Wrenn, 1999; Balk, Walker & Baker, 2010). 18.4 million students were enrolled in American colleges in 2009 (U.S. Census Bureau, 2009). That equates to more than 4.5 million college students who are grieving.[12]

10. "2017 Hurricane Harvey: Facts, FAQs, and how to help." World Vision.
11. "Marital status of the U.S. population, by sex 2018." Statista.
12. "College Grief & Actively Moving Forward (AMF)." What's Your Grief; "List of U.S. states by homicide rate." Wikipedia; "Murder map: Deadliest U.S. cities." CBS News.

PART TWO: USEFUL INFORMATION

With South Dakota having the lowest murder rate—1.4 per 100,000—and Louisiana having the highest rate—11.4 per 100,000—in 2018 in the United States,[13] the number of murders each year hangs around fifteen thousand. Approximately, 16,214 died by homicide in 2018.[14]

In 2018, in the United States, "there were an estimated 7,196,045 property crimes. The estimated numbers for all three property crimes showed declines when compared with the previous year's estimates. Burglaries dropped 11.9 percent, larceny-thefts decreased 5.4 percent, and motor vehicle thefts were down 3.1 percent."[15] "Collectively, victims of property crimes (excluding arson) suffered losses estimated at $16.4 billion in 2018."[16] Separate from the numbers, the emotional losses and the grief that comes from these losses are, no doubt, pose a challenge to our imagination. After all, the losses include personally precious items, such as grandfather's pocket watch or a computer full of irreplaceable photographs and other files.

The number of Americans getting some type of disability financial assistance check from the federal government is soaring. According to the Social Security Administration, "In December 2018, there were 9,919,094 people receiving Social Security disability benefits as disabled workers, disabled widow(er)s, or disabled adult children. The majority (86.1 percent) were disabled workers, 11.4 percent were disabled adult children, and 2.6 percent were disabled widow(er)s."[17] Individuals who suffer injuries and can no longer work may necessarily depend on financial support from others through the Social Security Administration. Clearly,

13. "FBI Releases 2018 Crime Statistics." Federal Bureau of Investigation—U.S. Department of Justice.

14. "FBI Releases 2018 Crime Statistics." Federal Bureau of Investigation—U.S. Department of Justice.

15. "FBI Releases 2018 Crime Statistics." Federal Bureau of Investigation—U.S. Department of Justice.

16. "FBI Releases 2018 Crime Statistics." Federal Bureau of Investigation—U.S. Department of Justice.

17. Social Security Administration. "Annual Statistical Report on the Social Security Disability Insurance Program, 2018."

BASIC FACTS ABOUT DEATH, LOSS, AND GRIEF

their loss of employment potential is considerable. Possibly, a number that surpasses the nearly ten million who receive financial assistance includes those who receive no financial assistance but who cannot be employed because of short-term disabilities.

More than ten thousand (10,000) individuals retire from active employment each day. While some celebrate their retirement and embark on years of successful and enjoyable retirement, others suffer losses (i.e., income, busyness, and personal identity) and grieve. "Majority of Retirees Say Their Standard of Living Has Stayed the Same. Sixty-four percent of retirees indicate their standard of living has "stayed the same" since they retired, while 25 percent say it has 'decreased.' Only nine percent say their standard of living has 'increased' since they retired."[18]

Many families suffer major loss, when a miscarriage occurs. The precise data for miscarriages are hard to determine. The following reported facts, though, surely indicate that a great deal of grief happens, based on current information. According to Hopexchange,[19]

- There are about 4.4 million confirmed pregnancies in the U.S. every year.
- 900,000 to 1 million of those end in pregnancy losses every year.
- More than 500,000 pregnancies each year end in miscarriage (occurring during the first 20 weeks).
- Approximately 26,000 end in stillbirth (considered stillbirth after 20 weeks)
- Approximately 19,000 end in infant death during the first month.
- Approximately 39,000 end in infant death during the first year.

---

18. TransAmerica Center for Retirement Studies. "A Precarious Existence: How Today's Retirees Are Financially Faring in Retirement, December 2018."

19. "Miscarriage Statistics." Hopexchange.

- Approximately 1 in 4 pregnancies end in miscarriage; some estimates are as high as 1 in 3. If you include loss that occurs before a positive pregnancy test, some estimate that 40% of all conceptions result in loss.
- Approximately 75% of all miscarriages occur in the first trimester.
- An estimated 80% of all miscarriages are single miscarriages. The vast majority of women suffering one miscarriage can expect to have a normal pregnancy next time.
- An estimated 19% of the adult population has experienced the death of a child (this includes miscarriages through adult-aged children).
- According to the Centers for Disease Control and Prevention, six million seven hundred thousand (6,700,000) women are infertile. For most women and the men who share their lives, the loss of hopes and dreams of having and rearing children evokes considerable grieving.(15) The Centers add that among women aged 15-44, 6.7% are infertile, 7.3 million have used infertility services, and 12.0% of women aged 15-44 have used infertility services.[20]

Conclusion

These facts provide merely a sampling of facts about death, loss, and grieving. As informative as these facts may be, they do not tell a complete story of loss and grieving. To these facts, almost everyone could add the kinds of losses that they have suffered. When parents feel the anguish of their son who is harassed and humiliated by his peers, they suffer loss. When children see their parents decline in health, they suffer loss. When many family members see a loved member succumb to torturous decline from substance abuse, they suffer loss. When a member of a family does not survive an automobile crash, the family members suffer the

20. "Infertility." Centers for Disease Control and Prevention

loss. The list of possible, major losses is a very long one. All of them should expand our awareness of grieving, beyond thinking narrowly about it as a result of death.

In fact, grief sometimes occurs before a loss. Commonly, this is referred to as "anticipatory grief." Many families can report that one of its members was ill for several months, if not longer, before the member died. Often, members of the family will observe, "We did a lot of our grieving before she died." The point of what they say is that in anticipation of the somewhat predictable loss, they grieved.

Anticipatory grief may be seen in families in which a member suffers extreme impairment. "Dad was still alive, but he really wasn't dad anymore." Dementia is a common form of losing a family member long before death occurs. With mixed feelings, including sadness, their loved ones often say things like, "I sit and talk with mom, but she doesn't know who I am." Among many other pictures of grief, this one captures serious loss and real grief.

What to Say to Grieving Friends

What we say to grieving friends may be less important than the fact that we are friends with the grieving person. It is friendship that gives us permission to be with the grieving friend and allows us to say what needs to be said.

Most of us have discovered that caring for a grieving person emerges from having a meaningful relationship with her/him. Without this relationship, very little that we say or do really matters. Saying anything to those who grieve comes from caring. The first and most important thing, then, is to say to them that you care. If you don't care, almost anything else you say or do doesn't matter much.

Caring for others when they grieve often comes as a welcome, but sometimes frustrating challenge. We want to "do something" to ease the pain that we know they carry, seeing that it is exhausting and sometimes burdensome for them. Even with the best of ideas about what to say, saying it face-to-face—in the face of acute loss and pain—never comes easily. The challenge comes from what the grieving person needs and not so much from what we may want to say to the grieving person. For example, with a newly widowed young woman, a good approach may be to direct her to eat—"You need to eat. So, let's sit down and have something together." However, with another newly widowed young woman, a good approach may be to follow her directions—"I'm ready to do whatever you need for me to do. If you want to get something to eat, just let me know. We'll go, whenever you're ready."

Keep in mind that communicating with a grieving person depends on your relationship with her/him, your sensitivity to grieving, and your considered discretion. Also, your history of grieving may be important, too. Saying just anything that comes to mind, based on your experience of grieving, may or not be helpful. When your history of grieving is supported by considered discretion and widely supported insights, such as those in this book, what you say to grieving others is much more likely to be helpful.

As you consider what you may say to a grieving friend, you may want to anticipate saying little or nothing. Often, your caring presence is more important than anything that you may say or try to say to a grieving friend. So, anticipate that saying nothing may be a wise approach to your grieving friend. Saying very little, but attending to a grieving person and listening with interest and compassion may be the best way to help.

Also, as you consider what you may say to a grieving friend, ask, "What do I know and understand about grief?" This question point to the necessity of studying grief so that you may say things to your grieving friend that are likely to be comforting, reassuring, and healing.

When it comes to grieving, easy comments to grieving persons are hard to find. Again, heartfelt caring is the necessary feature of saying almost everything to a grieving person. This chapter includes a long list of things that you may say to a grieving friend. It is unlikely that all of them will be useful for you. And, maybe, none of them will be useful for you. Our hope is that some of them will seem just right for you to communicate to a grieving friend, even if you have to re-word them so that they fit more closely what you want to say. So, after assuring her/him of your care, you may offer expressions of your caring in some of the following ways, when they are appropriate:

"Your grief will take longer than most people think. Be patient with yourself." At some time, you will hear grieving friends say something like this: "I still think about her, even after all this time. It amazes me that I'm still dealing with her death. And, it's not all bad. Some really good memories come to mind." In thinking about what you may say to a grieving person, prepare yourself to affirm statements like this.

"Your grief will take more energy than you would have ever imagined." Most people who grieve will come to recognize that they are tired, usually when they begin to recover their normal energy. It is at this time that they realize how very much energy they have used. Encouraging grieving friends to rest is a good thing to do, although many of them/us refuse to do this.

"*Your grief will involve many changes and be continually developing.*" Just imagine yourself laughing from a memory of the one who died and then feeling guilty for laughing. This may seem weird, but it is fairly common. In good and bad ways, grieving is an adventure.

"*Your grief will show itself in all spheres of your life, including emotional, social, spiritual, and physical aspects of your life.*" This makes sense, doesn't it? After all, loving relationships affect every aspect of our lives. Some of those whom we lose to death are ones with whom we share meals, money, vacations, children, and so much more. So, when we lose a loving relationship, all aspects of our lives are affected in new and demanding ways. The demands are almost too numerous to name. Just a few examples may make this clear. Following a loss, say, of a marital partner, the new demands may involve finding someone to mow the grass, locating a buyer for a car that is no longer needed, or finding ways to make sense of unexplained finances.

"*In many ways, your grief will depend on how you perceive your loss.* Some of how you perceive your grief may come from grief experiences that go back a long way in your life." For example, many families discover new ways of renewing their commitment to one another and loving one another. These families feel the pain of loss, but also re-discover the importance of their relationships and heartwarming fulfillment in these relationships. We can hope that this is a common discovery.

"*You will grieve for many things that are both symbolic and tangible, and not just the death of your special one.*" This may be seen in more ways than may be easily illustrated here. Nevertheless, just imagine a few ways that grieving may involve symbolic and tangible aspects of life. For example, a familiar table game, such as poker or Monopoly, that you played with your deceased partner may become associated with dread or sadness because of its connection with your deceased partner. Or, even friends that you shared with your deceased partner may be avoided because of their connection with your lost loved one. Similar connections may be made with objects, such as silverware, or places, such as church or even the home you shared. However, a grieving person may go in a direction that is opposite from what is described above. Because a familiar game is connected with the deceased love one, the bereaved person may carry very positive associations with it.

One of the more common but frequently unacknowledged sources of grief that becomes more profuond and enduring than many can imagine is the loss of the possibillity of having a child. Infertile couples often grieve the loss of something that is not tangible. For them, it is quite real, though. It is the death of a dream—the expectation that something very basic about life and completely desirable will not happen.

"You will grieve for what you have lost already and for what you have lost for the future." A necessary feature of grieving is that the grieving person anticipates what life will be like without the one who died. The bereaved person's future has and will change. To say this another way, "Your grief will entail mourning not only for the actual person you lost but also for all of the hopes, dreams, and unfulfilled expectations you held for and with that person, and for the needs that will go unmet because of the death." For many grieving individuals, this is the long, hard reckoning with loss.

"Your grief will involve a wide variety of feelings and reactions, not solely those that are generally thought of as grief, such as depression and sadness." The larger body of feelings and reactions for individuals who grieve may include relief, for example. A grieving widow began to travel almost immediately following the death of her husband because, according to her view of taking care of her very ill husband for almost three years, she needed to express her freedom to move and to enjoy new things. Another example is that a mourning brother worked hard for almost two years with anti-smoking campaigns because of his anger, due to the fact that his sister died from lung cancer that was very likely caused by smoking for forty plus years. The widow's urge to travel or the brother's anger toward cancer are the kinds of reactions that tell us how very personal grieving is. For each grieving person, feeling and expressing grief is unique.

PART TWO: USEFUL INFORMATION

"*Your loss will resurrect old issues, feelings, and unresolved conflicts from the past.*" Virtually all relationships are unfinished. For example, a common feeling is regret about not having expressed love enough toward the person who died. Another common kind of unfinished business is that grieving individuals reflect a lot about the shared ambitions that they can no longer consider. They may say something like, "You know, we always thought that we would just get in the car and travel throughout the Southwest, but we just never got around to it." More personally, though, grief sometimes requires us to face the sore and unresolved aspects of the now ended relationship. This is seen in the widower who says, "I could have made our lives much better than I did. She just tried harder than I did. Now, I see that."

"*You will have some identity confusion as a result of this major loss, due partially to the fact that you are experiencing reactions that may be quite different from reactions that you have had to other events.*" Generally, the closer we are to the person who died, the more tangled the grieving becomes. This should come as no surprise. Losing someone close to us is difficult, at best. Among the many possible expressions of confusion about her/his identity, an individual may say something like, "Since we first met, we were a pair. I never thought about what my life would be like without him, but here I am. Now, what do I do? I'm not sure who I am anymore."

"*You may have a combination of anger and depression, such as irritability, frustration, annoyance, or intolerance.*" Some of these unpleasant feelings may come from exhaustion. This is somewhat normal. In addition, though, grieving individuals often feel serious frustration with the challenges of adapting to life without the one who died. After all, they did not want this change. Like it or not, though, they must adapt. And, the range of demanded adaptation is very wide, including financial adjustments, eating with a change in partners or alone, and possibly relocating from one residence to another, and much more.

"*You will feel some anger and guilt or, at least, some manifestation of these emotions.*" At the time grieving individuals feel these things, the feelings are likely seen as large and very important. In the long run, they may seem small. However, the dread is that the long run may intensify these feelings so that grieving individuals believe—falsely or not—that they have permanently turned "sour." Most grieving individuals will feel these not-so-positive feelings and somewhat naturally move beyond them.

"*You may have a lack of concern about yourself.*" Many individuals who grieve push themselves in a somewhat gritty, hard-headed manner to get through the pain of grief, to the point of apparent self-neglect. However, as troubling as this may appear to be, it is generally not a long lasting pattern of behavior. Still, for those who care for the grieving person, self-neglect should get attention, while being placed in the context of intensely personal suffering. For example, a woman who knew of her serious cardiac problems became extraordinarily energetic when her mother died, placing her at great risk. Despite caution from others, she persisted in energetic care-taking of other members of her family. She survived, but caused considerable worry among those who cared for her.

"*You may experience grief spasms, acute upsurges of grief that occur suddenly with no warning.*" As confusing as it may be, the fact is that grief almost always has its "ups" and "downs." Grief is inconsistent. "Everything was going great. Then, I opened a book where my dad had left a love note to mom. It was emotional and beautiful. And I just lost it." Events like this are fairly common. Most of us who have lost someone close could report something like this: We are eating at a restaurant. We meet a friend whom we have not seen for a while. With no knowledge of our mother's death, the friend says, "Hey, how's your mom doing?" Understandably, we may feel a surge of pain.

"*You will have trouble thinking (memory, organization and intellectual processing) and making decisions.*" This, too, is somewhat unusual for an enduring pattern of behavior. When it happens, it us usually an isolated episode and often related to difficult decision making, such as selecting a coffin in which the deceased or making arrangements to move from a beloved home to another home. Sometimes, this difficulty is imposed on grieving individuals. For example, a widower stares helplessly at a stack of bills and family papers and says, "I don't know what to do. James always took care of these things. I don't know which ones have been paid or which accounts are closed or anything. I'm just lost."

"You may feel like you are going crazy." If you say something like this to a grieving person, it will likely be said because he/she wonders about whether he/she is going crazy. Moments of this kind of wondering are not unusual, although they are infrequent. Typically, they come in moments when the grieving person is unwary of being bereaved. So, you may hear him say something like this: "I came home. I micro-waved one of those frozen dinners. And, I'm sitting there at the table and hear a car. And, I think to myself, "Ah, there she is; it's about time she got home.' Then, I thought, 'Are you crazy or what?' She's not coming home. Ever. And I know that. I felt really weird."

"You may be obsessed with the death and preoccupied with the deceased." Many individuals become obsessed with loved ones who have died. For many, the loss is shocking to a degree that it occupies almost all of the thinking and energy of the bereaved. Allowing for great variability in the pace and durability of obsession with the deceased, for most individuals the obsession fades, just like the pain of grief. With unduly obsessed individuals, special care is needed. In addition, encouragement for them to seek professional help may be needed.

"You may begin a search for meaning and may question your religion and/or philosophy of life." With or without grieving, many individuals question their religion and/or philosophy of life. For them, such questioning often leads to elevated understanding and increased comfort with their religion. However, because a loss by death is intimately personal and painful, questions almost inevitably arise. You may want to encourage questions, simply because questions lead to answers. Sometimes awkwardly, the answers may be hard to accept. However, without hiding a painful experience with a happy mask, many individuals discover that their questions confirm that they have the strength, determination, and faith that they can handle difficult questions and answers. Yes, they

can find what many of have found through our grief: There is love in loss. There is strength in weakness. And, as odd as this may seem, the questions themselves often contain the answers. Asked long enough, many of their questions about life and death produce positive outcomes. Obviously, this is not the situation for everyone who grieves, but it is common.

"You may find yourself acting socially in ways that are different from before your loss. In doing this, you are attempting to piece together a new social life." During bereavement, almost all bereaved individuals need to re-negotiate their way or relating with others. The re-negotiation is a matter of degree. For the young widow, this may be pervasive and difficult. For the long-married couple who lose one of their elderly parents and who have siblings and a large social support system, this will not likely require extensive re-working of their social relationships.

"You may find yourself having a number of physical reactions that are unfamiliar to you." Most of us know that grieving is usually exhausting. Exhaustion is as much emotional as it is physical. So, physical reactions usually come with grieving. Fatigue is one of them. Other common reactions include tension, distressed stomach, sleeplessness or headaches. For most grieving persons, these appear during the most intense times of grieving and dissipate after the intensity has passed.

"You may find that there are certain dates, events, and stimuli that bring upsurges in grief." While grief reactions may come with certain dates, events, and other stimuli, these should not come as surprises. After all, a deceased person with whom we shared many aspects of our lives is connected in our memories with all of these aspects. So, a photograph of your deceased loved one's favorite actor may cause a reaction. Or, the afternoon sun on the lawn that your deceased loved one kept neatly mowed may trigger a reaction. And, then, there are reminders that are more directly associated with the deceased loved one, including birthdates, wedding anniversaries, or a special gift from the one who died.

"Your acquaintances will have unrealistic expectations about your mourning and may respond in ways that seem to you to be

inappropriate." Sometimes, those who love the grieving person create expectations that do not "fit." Usually, these expectations express good intentions. The grieving person may need someone to coach him/her to see these expressions as good intentions, even when they are inappropriate or even painful. For example, with the best of intentions, friends may strongly encourage the grieving person to resume certain social activities, such as meeting friends for lunch or going to church. A widow whose husband killed himself felt intense confusion, rejection, and humiliation because of his quite inexplicable suicide. She needed time to retire from normal activities, including going to church. Fortunately, those who had shared the widow's life for many years understood her need to withdraw from many of her normal activities and, when she was ready, welcomed her, including welcoming her to church.

"Certain experiences later in life may resurrect intense grief for you temporarily." Losses come in many forms. Any of them may be associated with the worst grieving that we have experienced. The loss of a job may be emotionally associated with the death of a parent or spouse, for example. Or, the departure of a beloved minister may be associated with other kinds of loss. Or, the death of a pet shared with a marital partner may evoke strong reactions, say, two or three years after the partner died. While these experiences may be confusing, they are understandable and normal. Also, this kind of reaction to loss of a job or a minister or a pet confirms that loss should be understood more broadly than loss that comes from the death of a loved one.

"Your grief will bring with it, depending upon the combination of factors, an intense amount of emotion that will surprise you and those around you." Quite apart from death and grieving, many events evoke emotions that surprise us. Getting a new job that had been long sought and deeply desired may evoke strong feelings, including some surprising ones. "I am saddened by moving on happily, without my wife." Similarly, leaving a house that has long been a place of many important family and personal relationships, such as bringing home a new infant, may evoke strong feelings.

The fact is that none of us can accurately predict how we will react to major life-changing events.

"Your expectations of yourself as grieving may be unrealistic, along with many inadequate responses from others that make judging your expectations somewhat more difficult." For most of us, grief is a fairly uncommon experience. We do not experience it frequently enough to know what to expect of ourselves. Because of this, our expectations of ourselves as grieving persons may or may not fit the circumstances of the death. An important factor is that all losses are not the same. For example, a grieving man reports his experience with losing his elderly mother. Mainly, he talks about how very grateful he is for his mother and his memories of her as a devoted, giving, and loving mother. In contrast, he talks about his brother's murder several years before his mother died. His feelings about losing his brother involve anger more than anything else. So, at any given time, grief may defy our best expectation about what it should be. Several factors may come into the death-related situation that affects grief. For those of us who help or want to help grieving friends need to consider the relationship of the deceased with the friend, the timing of the death (i.e., sudden or following a prolonged illness), the age of the deceased (i.e., elderly person or young child), cause of death (i.e., lung cancer, suicide, or accident, for examples),

"Your grief will surprise you as you see the range of expression of your grief." If individuals are asked about their expressions of grief, their responses may come as surprises. Of course, some will talk about feeling sadness and feeling lost. And, feeling angry about being "left behind" or about "being stuck with all these bills to pay." These feelings are not surprises. However, some individuals will report about feeling free, with their newly discovered freedom to do what they wish to do, without the constraints of having to care for the person who died. Or, others may report a new and exciting social life, as if their relationship with the now deceased individual kept them from having a thriving social life. Surprises during grief are almost inevitable.

PART TWO: USEFUL INFORMATION

"You will feel grief somewhat more intensely because of certain reminders of your loss, such as anniversaries, certain holidays, contact with mutual friends, finding special objects that the two of you valued." The need to escape from grief is understandable. It hurts. Nevertheless, after the most intense period of grieving during the few weeks following a death, inevitable and sometimes quite unexpected reminders of the death arise. These reminders take many different forms, such as a letter coming to the bereaved person's home, addressed to the deceased loved one. Or, a routine telephone call from the physician's office, reminding the deceased person of a scheduled appointment. Almost everyone has experiences in which awkward, if not painful, feelings of grief are evoked from the grieving person.

"Your grief is uniquely yours. It may or may not follow the pattern about which others tell you." One of the unfortunate communications that goes to grieving persons is something like this: "I remember when my _____ died. I decided that I needed to _____ _____ _____. You may want to do this, too. If you did it, I think you would be okay." This kind of communication misses the fact that grieving is not experienced in a universally consistent way. It varies a great deal from one person to another. It is deeply personal and unique.

"Of all the things you do or don't do with your grief, please remember that, above all else, your need for people goes on. Maintain your contact with people, especially people who care for you. Refuse to isolate yourself from others. You need them and they need you. Act on your need for them." One of the many temptations of grieving persons is to withdraw and grieve privately. This is quite okay. It is healthy, insofar as grief really is a private matter. However, sometimes, the need for privacy stretches into unnecessary isolation and loneliness. This can be a serious problem for bereaved individuals. For those of us who have interest in their well being, visiting with them, if nothing else, usually helps them to avoid prolonged isolations. If the prolonged isolation continues, different steps, such as seeking professional help, may be needed.

Note: Many of the main points in this discussion are adapted from Therese Rando's book, *How to Go on Living When Someone You Love Dies*. However, the elaborations on these points are additions that appear only in this book.

What NOT to Say to a Grieving Friend

So far, everything in this chapter aims to help you to know what to say to grieving friends. All of the things that you may say emerge from caring and genuine interest in your grieving friends. This is the way it should be. Sometimes, though, caring and genuine interest can be expressed in awkward, if not hurtful, ways. So, before leaving this discussion, let's take a look at things that you will not want to say to your grieving friends.

I know how you feel. Usually, this is neither a smart, sensitive, nor effective thing to say. When my grandmother—my "other mother"—died, my mother had just had a heart attack. When we received the news that my grandmother had died, my mother was being prepped for heart surgery. So, my grieving stood under the cloud of my mother's health risks. At the time of my grandmother's funeral, no one could have known how I felt, although a few individuals tried to assure that they had this knowledge.

To tell another person that you know how she/he feels carries the message and conclusion that you may know better than the other pereson how she/he feels. For example, what may another person feel about having a broken leg? And, what factors may shape feelings about having a broken leg? Let's consider a few variations on the theme of having a broken leg and the feelings that may come with each variation.

- Your neighbor slips on the ice on her front steps and suffers a concussion, along with a broken leg.
- Your neighbor suffers with a broken leg, following an automobile accident in which he was hit by a drunk driver and in which his wife suffered broken back.

- Your neighbor drank much too much on New Year's Eve, climbed to the roof of his home, fell to the ground, and broke his leg.

So, when it comes to the broken leg of each of your neighbors, do you know how she/he feels about having a broken leg? Probably, you do not know how each one feels, due to the complications of each of their situations. Grieving the loss of a loved one is generally much more complicated than having a broken a leg.

It's part of God's plan. Just imagine how you or I may respond to this message, say, if your or my spouse just died. Maybe, our thoughts would be something like this: "Really? God planned to throw tragedy into my life?" "Are you saying that God wants me to suffer?" "So, if you know God's plan for my life, what's the rest of the plan?"

The idea that death and grieving for your friend is part of God's plan has many similar ways of being said. Some of the other ways are these:

- This is what God wanted for you
- He's in a better place now.
- God will see you through this.
- This is God's will.
- Heaven has another angel, now.
- God never gives us more than we can handle.

Again, these messages usually come from good intentions. We want to say something that may be comforting. Before we say them, though, we should carefully consider how they may be heard and received by a grieving friend.

Don't worry; everything will be okay. Messages like this are fairly common. Grieving persons, though, are typically worried about many things. They are sometimes worried about whether they can survive the loss, their children, their own health problems, their finances, and many other things. So, why would we tell them not to feel what they feel?

How are you doing? While this is an understandable inquiry, it often misses the significance of intense grieving. Generally, during times of intense grieving, your suffering friends really do not know how they are doing. You may want to compare intense grieving to an individual's response to having major surgery. Immediately following surgery, even while the surgeon reports that the surgery went well, the patient usually feels much worse after the surgery than before the surgery. So, even when the surgery went well, the patient is quite unsure about how she/he is doing. The same is true with intense grieving.

Similar to the message, above, another one is this one: *Is there anything I can do for you?* Or, *is there anything you need?* The unfortunate implication of this question is that it suggests that, even in moments of intense grieving, the bereaved person should know what she/he needs. Usually, this is not what they know well. Instead, they know that they hurt and that they are confused about what life will be like in their future.

It was his/her time to go. So, what exactly is "his time" or "her time?" And, how would you know this? Unfortunately, this message often conveys the belief that the death should have inevitably happened at this time.

A Final Word about What to Say

When saying things to grieving persons, one of the most important lessons for me came at a funeral home. Visitation at the funeral home centered around a young woman who had been married only for two years when her husband died in an automobile crash. Along with my friend, Harvey, we stood in an informal line, with everyone reverently and patiently approaching the young widow, one after the other. She sat, obviously distressed.

Neither Harvey nor I paid much attention to what others said to the young widow. However, I believe that we heard, at least, two comments that others offered to the widow. One was "If you need anything, just call; I will help in any way I can." The other was "This is God's will; I will be praying for you." The voices of these two comments were quite sincere. Surely, the speakers intended to offer support for the widow.

When my friend, Harvey, approached the widow, he took her hand and said, "I know you hurt. And, you will be hurting for a while." He smiled in a gentle and affirming manner. And, in response to him, somewhat tearfully, she said, "Thank you. Thank you for understanding." And, even with tears, she smiled, too.

If telling grieving friends or family members what is most important for us to say and for them to hear, the most effective ways are known. Based on attuning our responses to the needs of friends or family members, these ways may be summarized in just a few sentences: Keep it simple. Keep it honest. Keep it real.

What to Do for Them When They Grieve

Grief is inevitable. Grief takes many forms. Grieving is highly individual. With these things taken into account, here are some suggestions for helping grieving friends and relatives.

Be sure to monitor your emotions. The importance of this is that you do not want to relate with your grieving friend in ways that serve your needs more than your friend's. Maybe, by asking yourself certain questions, you may be able to elevate your awareness of your emotions. Consider these questions:

- How comfortable am I with my memories of grieving?
- What do I know about the normal experience of grieving, quite apart from my personal experience with grieving?
- How familiar am I with miscarriage, suicide, job loss, retirement, and other grief-causing events?
- What is my level of confidence about being able to express support for a grieving friend, based on real experience?
- Do I have access to sources of helping grieving persons, apart from myself as a resource for a grieving friend?
- What are my personal skills that may help my grieving friend?

The list of possible questions could be much longer than this one. The point of the questions, though, is that careful self-examination and self-awareness are in themselves important assets in helping a grieving friend.

Think in very practical terms. Obviously, feeling concern for a grieving person is critically important. In addition, the common frustration and necessary consideration is "what to do." Concern is expressed somehow. So, considering the unique needs of your friend, what do you do? Again, think in very practical terms. When you think this way, you may want to

- Take food to your friend, a common and valued expression of caring

PART TWO: USEFUL INFORMATION

- Mow your friend's lawn
- Get needed items from the grocery store
- Take care of your friend's dog or cat
- Send a gift to your friend's preferred charity
- Send a card or write a note to your friend
- Gather funds for your friend
- Give blood on behalf of your friend
- Offer to answer the phone, while your friend rests or takes care of other business
- Coordinate the delivery of food or other gifts for your friend
- If your friend needs help with child care, offer this service

When your friend may need you, make yourself available. Demonstrate your commitment to your friend.

Listen carefully, without feeling compelled to give advice. Usually, your friend will need you to listen, instead of directing her/his grief. Listening is almost always a very good thing to do, mainly because grieving individuals often believe that no one can understand what they are feeling. Listening helps them to convey to others what they are feeling.

Avoid escapist ideas that inadvertently tell your friend that you have no clue about how to help. Escapist ideas include statements like "Your mother is in a better place now" or "God has called her home" or "If you have faith, there is no need to cry." Instead of succumbing to the temptation to suppress your friend's grief, consider ways to honor your friend's grief.

For example, can you help your grieving friend to identify selected memories or items of importance that need to be preserved? Is there a photograph that needs to be displayed? Is there an acquaintance of your bereaved friend who needs to receive an item of significance from the one who died?

Accept the likelihood that your grieving friend will show distress and express negative feelings. Yes, sometimes much to our discomfort, a widower may say, "These damn bills are driving me crazy. I have no idea how he paid the mortgage. Just look at all of this crap. How did he make any sense of it?" Moreover, allow your friend honestly to express real feelings that may emerge during grief. For many who care for grieving friends, they may confront a challenge when their grieving friend expresses anger or bitterness toward God. Allowing your friend to honestly express real feelings, especially in relation to real needs, can be extremely helpful. For example, in the case of a husband's death, does his widow need help with gathering disposable items and disposing of them? Does a widower need help with learning how to pay bills online? Does a surviving parent with young children need short-term help with child care?

Your grieving friend may show heightened ambivalence toward the deceased loved one or about the experience of grieving. While this is not typical of grieving, it is not unusual. Sometimes, this ambivalence may show itself in denials of the fact that a loved one has died. If this comes early in the grieving process, it likely indicates deep and anguished struggle to accept the loss. If it comes later, say, after a few months beyond the loved one's death, this likely indicates a serious problem. In response to early ambivalence, the better response is to show patience and support, with statements of encouragement about the painful process of grieving. In response to late ambivalence, the better response is to encourage your friend to seek professional help.

Again, prolonged denial is unusual. An example of this is seen in the story of a widower who bought her deceased husband an expensive desk, chair, and accouterments. Only through steady, positive and caring support, the widower sought professional help. With considerable pain and over a period of about a year, she emerged from her denial and affirmed the death of her husband and herself as a survivor.

Because grieving individuals feel isolated, as if no one could possibly understand their pain, comfort often comes through simple actions, such as hugs. For most grieving individuals touch is comforting and healing.

Above all, understand that grief is a normal and common reaction to serious loss. It is an experience to be lived, much more than a problem to be solved.

As a normal and common reaction to serious loss, grief should stimulate friends to invent ways to show compassion and kindness, remembering that it is one thing to suffer and quite another thing to suffer alone.

Almost anything that expresses genuine caring is good. If your grieving friend likes baseball games, buy tickets and go to a game. Or, if your grieving friend hasn't visited a favorite restaurant because she went there with her now deceased husband, maybe she would enjoy going there with her friend—you. Whatever you do, keep in mind that heartfelt bear hugs are always good. They usually say without words that you care. And, hugs are free. So, hug away!

PART THREE
GRIEF AND FAITH

Facing Grief with Faith

We grieve. It doesn't feel good. All of us know this. Many of us are well acquainted with grief. Still, despite its familiarity, we have questions about grieving.

What questions do you bring to grieving? If you are like many of the rest of us, you bring the questions that most of us bring. These are questions like these:

- What is grief? What is the best way to understand what happens to us when we grieve? How may we make sense of this intensely personal experience?
- Is grief good for us? As a natural response to loss, can we find good in being natural? If so, what is good grief?
- How do we know that we are grieving well or not so well? Are there signs that may help us?
- How does personal Christian faith speak to our grief? Does Christian faith play a real and significant role in grieving?

The information here aims to answer these questions and more. It's most basic goal, though, is to provide information about how to live through a grief experience with Christian faith. Those of us who deliver this information understand that none of us has complete and final explanations of your grief or our own. At least, grieving is complex—too complex for simple answers. However, it does not lie beyond understanding.

Obviously, we hope that the information here helps you. Whether it helps you as well as we would like for it to help is another matter. With this in mind, we hope to be as sensitive to you as we wish for you to be to those whom you seek to help. We invite you to reflect on your personal experience of grieving. So, as you read about grief, please give attention to your possible need to understand your personal history and experience with grieving. How have you handled important losses? Are there important memories of your grieving that cause you to feel anxious or dread about reading this material? What have you gained from your grieving that may be helpful for others? As you reflect on your gains from grieving, what would you most want others to gain from your experience?

As you begin to read this, you may want to consider whether you are ready to read it. If you are feeling acute pain because you are grieving, you may not want to read this at this time. Still, even if you are now grieving and you believe that you can reasonably focus on the material here, please read on. Because we have grieved, too, we hope that this is a helpful resource for you, with heartfelt sincerity.

Understanding Grief

The word "death" sounds like an ominous one. Whether we use the word or not, when someone we care about is threatened by death, we feel deeply about the prospect of loss. Almost always, we do not hear about death as something that feels good. Instead, when we anticipate the loss of someone we love, we anticipate hurt—or grief. Usually, with dread and foreboding, we wonder what life may be like without him or her.

Grief, then, is the hurt we feel, after an important personal loss. It is an emotional and physical reaction to this loss. Usually, when we think about grief, we think first about the death of someone we love. Surely, this is the most common kind of significant loss, but it is not the only one. Many individuals feel grief when they go through a divorce. Or when a pet dies, when a valued possession such as a wedding ring is lost, or when a home burns, people grieve. Grief comes to us in many different ways. For now, though, we are talking about the grief that comes when a loved person dies.

Just for clarity, something may need to be said about the difference between terms like "grief," "mourning," and "bereavement," because individuals are sometimes confused by them. In short, as indicated above, *grief or grieving* refers to the pain, hurt, and other internal disturbances that we feel, in response to significant loss. Usually, *mourning* refers to expressions of grief. So, we may speak about "mourning rituals or customs." Typically, *bereavement* refers to our separation from a loved one, with the most common bereavement coming because of death, with the emphasis on the period of time that follows loss. Maybe, a sentence that uses each of these words may help.

- "I could see the pain of *grief* in her eyes, in her face."
- "Usually, when people are *mourning*, we host a meal for the family."
- "He had a lot of visitors at his house during his *bereavement*."

Because many of us have lost a loved person to death, we know that we have a lot in common with others who have experienced the same loss. Here are some of the things that we have in common:

Grief is painful. It hurts. In fact, in the few days that follow a death, it hurts so much that we feel and think of almost nothing else. We are more aware of the tightness in our throats than feeling ordinary hunger. We are more aware of a disturbed stomach, or even nausea, than our need to sleep. We feel uneasy, sometimes wondering whether a disease of some sort may have afflicted us. We see ourselves sighing deeply or breathing in unusual ways or muscle twitches that we have not seen or noticed before. We feel concentrated on our loss, as if our loss has taken over our lives. These things make us wonder what's happening to us, but they are normal. If you are grieving now, you may be feeling some of these things or other things that remind you of your loss.

Grief is directional. We move naturally through several stages, from acute pain to acceptance to feeling much like our former selves. If you are feeling acute pain at this time, you will come to feel better, although this may be hard to believe. Your pain itself may simply be a sign of feeling normally about a significant loss. Keep in mind, too, that people almost never get stuck in the pain of grieving, although feeling stuck is common. After all, when we feel something as intensely as grief, we give attention to it because it requires attention.

PART THREE: GRIEF AND FAITH

While grief is directional and may involve several stages, please ignore the impulse to oversee your direction and stages too carefully. This impulse may cause you to over-manage your grief, instead of living though it in a natural and healthy manner.

Grief is personal. If you are grieving, you know that grief is personal. You feel grief your way, not exactly like anyone else. Your feelings and your unique loss may be shared with others, but no one feels your feelings exactly the way you do. And no one thinks about it exactly the way you think about it. This is important, but do not let it separate you from others who have lost the same person that you have. Even if they do not experience grief exactly the same way you do, they either are experiencing it now or have experienced it in the past. Many people you know understand grief because they have felt it and worked through it. They can help you. Let them. Instead of letting your very personal feelings of loss separate you from others because they are not feeling grief as acutely as you are, let them help you to recognize that others have experiences losses similar to yours and may be helpful for you.

Grief is personal, to be sure. It is seldom an isolated experience, though. So, let yourself be cared for, as you grieve. Just as you wish for others to let you care for them when they grief, you may want to consider doing the same for them.

Grief moves slowly. For many people who lose a loved one to death, time seems almost to stop. The familiar markers that tell them that life goes on are not very important, immediately following a loss. A job, a bank balance, making new friends, planning a vacation, watching a football game on television, and other common aspects of life to which we give attention during normal times don't get attention at all, when grief is felt most deeply. Logically, we know better, but time seems to stop or, if not stop, to move very slowly. If you are grieving, you may not feel that your time is moving slowly. If you do, this is normal. You may want to remind yourself that grief moves slowly. It is the moving that is important. It says that, sooner or later, your life will resume the pace that it had before your loss. You may notice that your feelings today are not quite as intense as they were yesterday. Those who are acquainted with grief can affirm this for you.

Whether your grief seems to move slowly or not, the pace of your grief is yours. Grieving at your pace is important. While you can—and maybe should—learn from the grieving experience of others, you will grieve at your pace, not theirs.

Likewise, you may grieve in a manner that doesn't look like the grieving of others. For example, looking at an earlier part of this book, "Useful Information about Helping Grieving Friends," you may want to read about the things you may say or do for grieving friends and ask how many of these things may be helpful to you as you grieve.

Grief is more than hurt. The hurt of grief is the most common feeling. If you ask anyone what it feels like to grieve, almost universally you will hear, "It hurts." If you were to ask more questions about feelings, you would hear about other ones. You may hear references to relief or confusion or, maybe, guilt or hostility. These feelings are normal, too, although sometimes they don't seem like it.

Many individuals who have cared for a critically ill family member for a long time, say, two years, and have seen their family member suffer usually know that "it's time to let go." After death, they are often relieved to know that their loved one is no longer suffering. This is normal. As a loving response to the end of suffering by our loved one, we may feel relief, too, as if our suffering has also ended. And, while grief hurts following death, we can also remind ourselves of the loving attention that we gave to the one we lost. At death, their pain is gone. And, we did all we could do to ease their pain. Grief hurts, but having done all we could do is reason for us to feel relieved, too.

Guilt often comes up, too. People who grieve sometimes say things like this:

- "If I had been more attentive to what she needed, she would still be with us."
- "I know that I should have taken him to the hospital long before I did."

- "I still wonder whether we found the right doctor. I should have done more."

When someone close to us dies, why wouldn't we raise questions about what happened? Raising questions is not necessary, but it is normal and understandable. We know how we second-guess ourselves when we lose a key or a bill that we should have paid or any number of other things. So, given the much higher importance of losing a loved one to death, why wouldn't we raise questions about what we may have done right or wrong? Mostly, as uncomfortable as they are, these questions are signs of love. These questions tell us that we wish with all our hearts that we could have done more than we did. This is the way love works, always wanting to do the good and right things for those who are loved. Moreover, following the loss of someone close to us, we usually have a lot of questions about how life is going to work in their absence. Loss requires adjustments, with some of them being painful and difficult and others being fairly easy ones.

Hostility or anger is a more challenging feeling. When loss is experienced as an insult, we are offended. We ask, "Why did this have to happen to me. My life was great. Now, it's not worth living." Even when hostility or anger is not as obvious as this, it may pop up. After all, following the loss of a loved one, numerous adjustments must be made. These adjustments are at least a nuisance and at most life-changing. For example, consider the man who loses his wife. Now, he must take care of everything, without her assistance. Now, the children are his exclusive responsibility. Now, the bills fall on him, along with getting back into church life, saving for the children's college expenses, maintaining the home, and on and on, not to mention the acute loneliness that usually sets in for a while. Why not be a little angry, in carrying all of these burdens without the love and support of a partner?

Your grief may not include guilt or anger. This is okay. The bigger point is that grief is more than hurt or sadness. These other feelings are normal, too. If you have them, you are likely as normal as everyone else who has experienced them.

While the feelings guilt and anger are uncomfortable, they give only parts of the picture of grieving. If you listen to grieving friends or relatives speak about their losses, you will hear many life affirming comments. Among many comments, they may sound something like these:

- "I just feel so blessed to have had him in my life."
- "I really miss my sister, but I am so grateful that we shared so many things.
- "No one taught me as much about life as my mother. She made my life good.
- "He was my anchor—my hero. I have so many wonderful memories."

Is Grief Good?

Is grief good? The shortest answer is "Yes." The longer answer is that it takes a lifetime to answer. For now, though, let's consider something in between "Yes" and the rest of your life.

Grief feels bad, but it is natural and healthy. Grief is a response to a real and significant loss. Feeling bad does not make grief good. It is feeling bad because of the loss of someone you love that makes it good. Grief is an affirmation of love. Without love, a genuine attachment to someone else, the loss of someone else would not be felt as important. With love, loss is always important. With love, loss means grief.

At any specific point in time, though, grief may seem to be "crazy." When you consider your grief, you may have some of the following thoughts.

- "What's wrong with me? I can't think about her without getting choked up. I just can't. I miss her too much."
- "You should see me when I eat. I may look like I'm enjoying it, but I'm just going through the motions. I'm not enjoying

it. It doesn't taste like anything to me. That's the way life is for me, now."

- "Am I crazy or what? I talk to him as if he's there beside me."
- "I'll be walking around the house. Then, I see something—her chair, her picture, her glasses, or whatever—and I lose it. I guess I haven't really accepted my loss. I feel like this is going to go on forever."
- "I wonder whether I'm being disrespectful. I talk about him like he was a stranger. You know, without much feeling. I guess I'm finally moving out of the darkness of pain. I just don't hurt as much, now."
- "I find myself wondering whether I really cared. And I shake my head and bring myself back to reality. He would want me to move on. You know, caring and remembering, but not living in the past."
- "Oh, you'll never know how funny she could be. I have hundreds of stories. It's almost irreverent, now. But she left a lot of us with a lot of funny memories. That's what I mostly remember about her."

Obviously, these statements tell us about many different reactions to significant personal loss. Are they normal, though? Are they healthy? Yes, they are both—healthy and normal. Some of them may appear to be strange, but they are normal and healthy. Also, they say a great deal about the process of grief. Grief moves through a process so that at one time a person may be paralyzed and at another time may be enjoying the memory of the one who died. This also says something about the stages through which grieving person pass. As you consider these stages, remember that your way of moving through them may not be just like anyone else's. Your movement may not carefully resemble the stages that are described here.

The fact is that many variables affect movement through these stages. Consider your thoughts about these various circumstances. One, a seventy-six year old man dies, after losing vision and hearing and after suffering with an illness for several years. Two, a thirty-two-year-old mother of three dies in an automobile accident. Three, a thirteen-year old girl hangs herself, following rejection by her girlfriends. Four, a twenty one year old man is murdered because another young man was interested in the same young woman. Five, a flash flood took the lives of the entire family—mother, father, and two children. While everyone who loved these individuals grieved, the process of their grieving may be complicated by some of these events, such as suicide or murder.

For most of us, grief is more or less intense and more or less complicated by the depth of our relationship with the deceased person, his age, and our belief about his relationship with God, and probably many other things that are unique to the relationship between the deceased and those who survive. Allowing for things that may make grief a complicated process, here are some commonly identified stages of grief. You may want to keep in mind that each of us moves through these stages in unique and personal ways.

Loss shocks those who lose. The chances are that if you are reading this, you are not experiencing shock. Shock means that the individual has heard that someone died and is emotionally stunned. Shock is being stunned. Shock does not allow us, say, to sit calmly and read a newspaper. The one who is shocked may behave in ways that, in looking back at them, seem strange.

A couple is having dinner. The knock on their door is followed by the news of their son's death. She goes back to the table, as if she may not have heard the news. After a few minutes, she stands, screams, and sobs uncontrollably. Her response is not unusual. It indicates that her personal life was altered to such an extreme that she could not immediately make sense of the change. She was overwhelmed and, instead of looking at her loss straightforwardly, she resumed doing what she was doing before the knock on her door. As strange as her behavior may appear, it is a normal reaction to overwhelming news. She showed shock. At least momentarily, this is utter disbelief that such an overwhelming event has occurred.

Another stage of grief is numbness. This means that, instead of absorbing the loss and making the necessary adjustments that the loss requires, the individual "goes through the motions." Feelings seem to be frozen. Sometimes action is frozen, too. The grieving person is confused by this response. "Why can't I get things done? This just isn't like me." Or, "I can't seem to get a grip on the situation. I can't think. I'm going in circles." Numbness, too, is a normal response to overwhelming loss. Typically, it lasts a fairly short time, following the death of a loved one. Simply put, it is the mind's and body's way of protecting itself. For a short time, it suspends the necessity of going on with life.

If you are experiencing numbness, you are not likely reading this. If you are reading this and experiencing numbness, you are likely wondering about the seeming unreality of what is happening to you. You wonder whether what you know to be true is really true. You feel tempted to deny what you know to be true and confused by this temptation. This is not denial. It is a phase of grief, a time during which the loss is not yet accepted as final.

Another major phase of grief is a struggle between fantasy and reality. Those who are acquainted with grief remember moments when they wished that the death had not occurred and tried hard to believe that it had not happened. "After I finish my shower and brush my teeth, I go to the kitchen, just like I always have. And, you know what, I really expect him to be there. He's always there. But he isn't there anymore. That's hard to accept." Or, "When I'm shopping for groceries and I hear kids laughing, I turn to look because I expect to see my little girl there. I know it sounds crazy, but that's what I do." Often this struggle includes times when grief seems to have evaporated and other times when grief seems to have taken over one's life. One is relief and the other is confusing. Both, though, are parts of a phase of grief that is quite normal.

Maybe, you find yourself doing what you have always done. You get the newspaper and put it where he sits and reads it when he gets home. And then you see yourself doing this and wonder what's wrong with you. As peculiar as this behavior or your own may seem, it is often an indicator of how much you wish that your loved one were still with you and that you are continuing to struggle with major adjustments in your life.

The important thing for you to hear is that this struggle between fantasy and reality is normal. Whether you just think about wishing your loved one had not died or act on the wish, such as placing the paper by his chair for him, your behaviors are normal. They are ways of struggling to accept the reality of your loss and to integrate this reality into your life.

Another major phase of grief is release. The loss is real. There is no way to hide it or to pretend that it isn't true. The pain is real. It cannot be denied. The loss and the pain express themselves. You cry. In your own way, your feelings pour out. You feel stuck with big feelings. You may feel like you can't get control of your feelings, as if they somehow have a life of their own. You look at yourself and think that your life is one long "ouch." You feel like the pain just won't stop.

Most people get to this time in a day or two, but your time to feel the loss may take weeks. This is not a problem. There is no standard way for you to grieve. There is no schedule you should follow. So, you release your feelings. This is simply a time during which all the things you have not known how to express come out. This is okay. Let your feelings go.

Oddly, while you feel a lot of pain and feel it deeply and constantly, the release of your feelings leaves you feeling much better. Also, the physical pain—fatigue, listlessness, and more—subside, too. The tightness in your throat goes away, along with other common physical complaints, including headaches or sleeplessness.

You may feel like a social misfit during the phase of release. After all, almost everyone else you know is not releasing feelings. Keep in mind that your feelings are real and that they will come out in some way. Keep in mind, too, that those who try to tell you not to release your feelings are not giving you good advice. "Don't cry, you will be okay." "Let God have your tears; you don't need them." If you need to cry, cry. Expressing grief is not an affront to God; it is an acknowledgment of your love of life, just as God loves life. Just as

PART THREE: GRIEF AND FAITH

God loves life, He also loves every one of our personal expressions of life, including our expression of painful feelings.

Another major phase of grief is learning to live with memories. Ken Doka says, "The lessening of grief is not the end of memory or attachment; death does not end a relationship."[21] Many grieving persons believe that when they begin to remember enjoyable, pleasant, funny times that they had with the one who died, they have betrayed the one they lost. Not so. Instead, this is an important sign that the grieving person is beginning to regain a reasonable and balanced memory of the one who died, instead of holding only a sad and painful memory. It is a sign of beginning to resume some of the normal routines of life.

Usually, learning to live with memories shows itself in enjoying a meal—really enjoying it—and thinking about the one you lost, even if you feel a surge of pain. It is going back to work and getting work done, without being preoccupied with your loss. It is going back to church, seeing familiar people, pews, and other things, and feeling good about being there, even if again you feel occasional episodes of pain. It is receiving a Christmas card for the one who died, causing you a momentary stab of pain and a pleasant recollection of the sender of the card and of the one who died.

Learning to live with memories goes from seeing yourself flooded with memories to seeing yourself simply enjoying remembering. This is a way of saying that from the beginning of your loss to a time when life looks pretty good again, you move from a time when the balance tilted in the direction of sore and raw memories to a time when the balance is tilted in the direction of liking to remember the one who died and enjoying reminiscing about the lost one with others who knew him or her. From one side of the balance to the other takes a long time. After a while many reminders of the one who died are welcome. So, when people ask about your loss and the one who died, you are quite comfortable hearing their questions and giving them answers. When you go places—work, a favored restaurant, church, visiting relatives, the symphony, vacation home, or wherever—that

21. Doka, "What Is Grief?"

remind you of the one you lost, you are okay with the memories. Eventually, you come to a time when you enjoy talking about your memories of the one you lost to death.

Finally, grief brings you to acceptance and affirmation. Having come this far, you are ready to accept your loss, even embrace it, and to affirm life. You recognize that memories of your loss bring gratitude, without stabbing pain. You talk about the one you lost and appreciate the relationship for what it was, without wishing unrealistically that it could be restored. You feel a renewed confidence in life, as if you have concluded that you can go on with life and that you will be okay. While exuberant hope may not be what you feel, the expectation of getting there is close to what you feel. You may wonder about how you could have felt so bad, during the worst times of your grief, but believe that life is for living and that living well is what you will do.

A part of living well is getting back into life. For many of us, this means that we begin to do things with others. It is helping your study group at church make pies for a Christmas celebration at church. It is going to the beach with your children, without your spouse. It is helping a neighbor to pour a concrete patio. It is sponsoring a wedding shower. It is deciding not to go to the cemetery and feeling okay with your decision. Getting back into life seems to be less and less of a challenge, as if your loss has taught you to appreciate life in a way that is more meaningful than you had before your loss. Whether you use these words or not, you are inclined to think, "Life is good."

This is not at all typical of grieving, but some people do not make it through the process of grief. Some do not recover from loss. Some try to go on with life, denying that the loss has occurred and building an increasingly morbid view of life. Others withdraw from life, afraid to take reasonable chances on life. Others become bitter, thinking that their loss is a kind of sick punishment against them. Others maintain hostility, as if life has cheated them. Others use their loss to solicit prolonged sympathy from their loved ones and other helpful individuals, such as pastors or therapists or neighbors. All of these individuals combined represent a small minority of persons who grieve. If you believe that you may have one of these problems, please consult with a professional person who can help you. This may be your minister or a mental health professional. Don't prolong your deep discomfort. Get help. Life can be much better than you are letting yourself make it.

Take another look at the stages of grief. Keep in mind that the stages are not inevitable. They are common, but not universal. And, please, learn what you can from these stages that may help you, but do not become fixated on these stages, as if you must determine where you are in grieving. Instead, grieve in ways that are real and honest for you.

Death, Grief and the Christian Hope

Death seems to many of us to be a kind of phantom invader, attacking us and making us feel extremely vulnerable, even when we have anticipated our loss. Death seems to ride thunderously into our quiet lives and leave us feeling pain, as if love, including the love of God, may not be real. Phantom or not, quiet or not, death is real. Our loss is real. And we hurt. You should never think that you should have to justify the pain of loss, any more than you have to justify the pain that comes when you drop a book on your toe.

Sometimes, though, we have questions. Along with the rest of us, you ask, "Why?" and no one seems to have the answer. You feel deep hurt, and no one seems able to ease your pain. And now, as you read this, wanting something that will clear away some of the mystery and maybe ease your pain. The answers to your questions must be important and real for you. Others cannot tell you how to grief or how to make sense of your grief. Maybe, though, as a way to begin to connect your experience with Christian hope, consider the prayer, below. Even if it seems to offer hints of sarcasm, it represents a man's attempt to reconcile himself to the death of his wife and to affirm life.

> Dear God,
>
> I have noticed death.

Or, maybe, I should say that death noticed me.

No, not noticed. Stared me down. And, I blinked first.

You may know that I would be quite content to avoid death altogether, but I don't seem to have this option. Death came and I lost.

So, I have noticed death. And, I have noticed your endurance of death.

I know about the cross.

Now, I lack the words to say more. What could I say? Death came to you and you lost, too. So, what could I say?

"Man, I bet that hurt?"

Or, "Sure, it was bad, but that was a long time ago?"

Or, "It was a cruel death, but, hey, everybody has to die sometime?"

Or, "Was it sacrifice or self-serving?"

Or, "It was okay, but God can do whatever he wants?"

Or, "I don't care?"

Or, "What a way to go; it got everybody's attention?"

Or, "Hey, get over it; you are God, after all.

Or, "Too late for me to cry about it."

Well, Lord, I have said all those things. And more.

But, then, I noticed death.

Or, should I say that death noticed me.

Your death. Your death noticed me.

In anticipation of my birth, your death noticed me.

Once I recognized the truth—that you died for me—

I lacked the words to say more. Amen.

If you are reading this, you have an interest in trying to understand life and death in the context of Christian faith. You are not alone. Many of us have looked at death and faith. We have many questions and probably have many of the questions that you have. We are not likely to answer all of your questions, but in an effort to cover some of the more important ones, here are some of our answers.

The Christian faith affirms death and grief as a part of life. The Christian faith sees death in two ways, as the cessation of life and as alienation from God. The threat of death, with both its meanings, is the basis of God's action in providing a means of salvation. Salvation through Jesus Christ is offered to save us from sin and death. Thus, as paradoxical as it seems, if there were no death, there would be no hope. Why would hope be considered or needed, if there were no death? So, at the heart of the Christian faith is the clear affirmation of God's love for us, including His tender and enduring denial of death as a barrier to life.

The Christian church is an affirmation of life. Your church brings life out of death. Your church says to you, "We stand with you in believing that God is the source of life. We comfort you in your grief. We provide caring and supportive relationships for you. We acknowledge your value as a person. We say to you that honesty, truth, caring, worship, serving others, and commitment are important to us, even in the face of death. These values are alive in you. Your values have not been destroyed by your loss." This is affirmed in Scriptures, "We know that we have passed out of death unto life, because we love each other." (1 John 3:14, NIV).

Hope is found in relationship with God. This is the heart of our shared faith. As the prayer above suggests, death calls our attention to a careful consideration of God in our lives. For many of us, this consideration leads to the conclusion that God loves us. When we grieve, this is not always clear to us, especially when pain is felt most deeply. As often as not, our pain is the most obvious feature of our lives, at least for a while. Sooner or later, though, after intense pain begins to fade, we look at life differently.

With Jesus, we feel the anguished cry, "My God, my God, why have you forsaken me" (Matt 27:46, NIV). But, also, we feel his acceptance of death, "Father, into your hands I commit my spirit" (Luke 23:46, NIV). His leap of faith is much like ours. Because of

God's love, we can claim hope in the face of death and when we feel grief. It is a leap of faith that may be risky, just because it is a leap, but not leaping is a much bigger risk. Hope—and the chance of landing in the warmth of God's eternal embrace—beats cynicism and despair. Giving life and death to God is better than succumbing to accepting the idea that we have been forsaken, with death being the proof.

During the most intense pain of grieving, most religious messages are hard to hear. This is understandable. Transcending pain, though, is the belief that neither death nor grief can separate us from God's love. In this inseparable relationship with God, there is hope, hope that requires a leap of faith, despite the hurt of grief.

> Who shall separate us from the love of Christ? Shall trouble or hardship or persecution or famine or nakedness or danger or sword? As it is written: "For your sake we face death all day long; we are considered as sheep to be slaughtered." No, in all these things we are more than conquerors through him who loved us. For I am convinced that neither death nor life, neither angels nor demons, neither the present nor the future, nor any powers, neither height nor depth, nor anything else in all creation, will be able to separate us from the love of God that is in Christ Jesus our Lord. (Rom 8:35-39, NIV)

Nothing can separate us from the love of God. Both in this life and in the life to come, this is the substance of our hope, the heart of our faith, the outcome of our belief, and the security of our acceptance. And, allowing us to live well, it is our gritty affront to death—our refusal to believe that death is the end of everything.

So, in your grief even now, you are alive. You may cry as much as you crave life. You may play as much as you pray. You may laugh as much as you labor. You may hurt more than you help. In all of this, and in everything else, God loves you. Grief and God are compatible experiences. In your grief, God finds you. Just as loving persons, such as members of your family or neighbors or ministers, surround you, God's love surrounds you, too.

PART THREE: GRIEF AND FAITH

Hope is found in desiring life. Even in the face of death, our desire for life cannot be denied, but in truth may be even more deeply felt. This desire cannot in itself confirm that there is life beyond life. No one can give us this assurance, based on her/his desire or it, no matter how sincere the desire may be. However, believing that life truly matters to you means that numerous specific actions from you can help you to find life and meaning for yourself—and possibly life beyond life.

To be clear, your personal faith may confirm your expectation that Heaven awaits you. This is a matter of faith, though, and not a factual confirmation, even if it feels like a factual confirmation. Beyond this faith and feeling, is there more that you may do to ensure that life beyond life awaits you? The short answer is "Yes."

In the movie, "Risen," a Roman official is dispatched, for the purpose of determining what happened after Jesus died. Did he rise from the dead? Was he still preaching and performing miracles? Skeptical of his findings, he showed intense confusion, when he encountered Jesus. He acknowledged that he was confused, while being drawn to Jesus. In a private conversation with Jesus, the skeptical Roman official said,

"I saw you die. When you died, I was there. I was present. I was there. I helped."

He acknowledged to Jesus that he helped Jesus to die. At the risk of seeming to be more dramatic than the question is intended to be, the question is, "Are you helping Jesus to die?" Maybe, a little explanation is needed.

Toward finding life and meaning for yourself, consider Jesus' way of describing the arrival of the Kingdom of Heaven.

> When the Son of Man comes in his glory, and all the angels with him, he will sit on his glorious throne. All the nations will be gathered before him, and he will separate the people one from another as a shepherd separates the sheep from the goats. He will put the sheep on his right and the goats on his left.
>
> Then the King will say to those on his right, "Come, you who are blessed by my Father; take your inheritance, the kingdom prepared for you since the creation of the

world. For I was hungry and you gave me something to eat, I was thirsty and you gave me something to drink, I was a stranger and you invited me in, I needed clothes and you clothed me, I was sick and you looked after me, I was in prison and you came to visit me."

Then the righteous will answer him, "Lord, when did we see you hungry and feed you, or thirsty and give you something to drink? When did we see you a stranger and invite you in, or needing clothes and clothe you? When did we see you sick or in prison and go to visit you?"

The King will reply, "Truly I tell you, whatever you did for one of the least of these brothers and sisters of mine, you did for me." (Matt 25:31–40, NIV)

Hunger. Thirst. Stranger. Sickness. Imprisoned. Nakedness. Responding to these real human needs is a way to affirm the importance of life to you and to get close to God, according to Jesus. The idea is as simple as it is important. "When you did it to one of the least of these my brothers and sisters, you were doing it to me!"

Hunger? Thirst? Strangers? Sickness? Imprisoned? Nakedness? So, who are "the least of these my brothers and sisters" in your world? Who are they?

> Is she the beggar in the parking lot of the grocery where you shop?
>
> Is he the widower who shows exhaustion and worry about his young children?
>
> Is he the alleged sex offender who faces criminal charges?
>
> Are they the couple who lost their home in the flood?
>
> Are they the parents of a heroin-addicted son about whom they are terrified?
>
> Is he the old man living alone and who can't see well enough to pay his bills?
>
> Is she the child who aspires to higher education but cannot afford to go?

Is she the cancer-afflicted, single mother who worries about what will happen to her children?

Is he the hostile neighbor who seems to push everyone out of his life?

Is she your ex-minister who suffers with major depression and isolation?

Where are the hungry, the thirsty, the strangers, the sick, the imprisoned, and the naked in your world? And, in response to them, what may you say or do?

One way to know God and to find hope is to find "the least of these" and respond to their needs. Responding to their needs is service to others, but also service to God. Service to others is not the only way to find Christian hope.

Attending to the needs of "the least of these" recognizes that the least of these may be you or me. It recognizes that all of us are vulnerable to hunger, thirst, being strangers, suffering sickness, and nakedness. While these things are unlikely to afflict most of us, we could be the widower who shows exhaustion and worry about his children or the couple that lost their home in a flood of the parents of a heroin addicted son or the older person who cannot see very well. More than imagining that we could be one of these, we are, in fact, among "the least of these." Yes, to be sure, you and I will endure suffering. And, at almost any moment in our lives, you or I could easily be among the neediest, if, say, the person whom we love more than life itself dies. Yes, grief makes us needy.

A Blessing for You

For now, as you grieve, my prayer for you is that your faith community reaches out to you and that you allow them to care for you. My prayer for you is that you allow God to find you, that you feel His presence, and that hope sustains you. When you allow God to find you, neither of you will be surprised by the fact that your grief is painful. It is. However, as painful as it is and as much as this should be recognized, there is more to grief than this. Grief is painful because it tells us how much we value life. And, because we value life, we will almost inevitably find ways to affirm and enjoy life, after grieving.

PART FOUR

GRIEVING AND BEYOND: ENCOURAGING STORIES

To Cope with Hope

I LIVED WITH YOUR dying for a long time. At first, I believed that we were looking at an illness, one of those things that distracts us from the really important other things we do. It was a nuisance back then. While I was concerned about you, I really was irritated by the inconvenience of having to help you with your appointments and treatments. I figured back then that if you were strong, you would take care of yourself without my help. I concluded that I would help you to be weak and overly dependent, if I did for you what you could do for yourself.

But you stayed sick. I noticed your change of color. I looked at your eyes as they changed from clear, clear and bright eyes to blurred, sad and tired eyes. I saw you begin to move uneasily, stumbling instead of transitioning gracefully from one place to another. I supported you as you walked, because you lacked the stamina to make it on your own.

My irritation changed to concern. I became scared at the prospect that this may be an illness from which you may not recover. You seemed to be more interested in fighting the illness than in knowing that your life may be at risk.

And when it became clear to me that your life was at stake, nothing else mattered. Job. House. Money. Sex. Lawn. Retirement. Vacations. Nothing mattered, except you and your life.

I felt guilty. How could I have missed the significance of your illness? I did not have the luxury of attending to my guilt. It was not important. Your illness was not about me. It was about life, your life. So, I joined the battle as best I could.

Our best efforts, though, could not sustain you. Maybe, you know the catastrophic tangle of despair that I felt without you. Maybe, you know how lost I was. Maybe, you know that nothing had meaning to me without you. Maybe, you know how I could not sleep or think about going on without you, without feeling guilty. I needed so much for you to know and to understand.

I shall never forget you. How could I? How does a man forget the love of his life. The person for whom he lived? The woman whose companionship gave his life meaning? The woman whom he adored? The shared dreams that will never come true? The one with whom he expected to live for another forty or forty-five years or so?

These questions are pretty well settled, now. I shall never forget you, but the questions no longer gnaw at me every day, and certainly not all day long. The questions still come up, but not every day.

The struggle goes on. It is different now, though. I no longer want to build a shrine to you and to worship you there. I no longer visit you at the cemetery, as I once did. I no longer feel guilty for laughing. I am giving myself enough slack to enjoy, really enjoy, a meal, without feeling guilty. The guilt is gone, but the love is not. The guilt is gone, but my life is not. I am alive.

As I continue to live, new struggles arise. To be sure, despair no longer has a grip on me. You certainly would not have wanted me to live my life in despair. I remind myself of this and of how you would want me stop hurting and to nurture life. I believe that you would want me to enjoy life. I remind myself of this, too. Now, without despair and with serious doses of enjoyment, I wonder how I can cope with hope? Without you, how do I cope with hope?

Ms. Nurse

Ms. Nurse, a competent and caring professional, demanded of herself that she measure up to high standards. She preferred perfection and received rewards that accompany such a preference. Thus, just as she delivered routine services to hospice patients and their families, she delivered her impeccable services to Mrs. Susan Purveys, a hospice patient and her husband, Sam, her primary caregiver.

Ms. Nurse explains the forms that she must complete. She maneuvers Mrs. Purveys so as to complete the physical examination that admission procedures require and explains every move she makes. She explains patient rights to Mr. and Mrs. Purveys. She explains the role of her attending physician. She explains the benefits of the hospice program, including the services of nurses, home health aides, chaplains, social workers, volunteers, and others. She explains the fees arrangement that comes with the Medicare Hospice Benefit.

Sam speaks. He says that he loves Susan as much now as he did when he married her fifty three years ago. Ms. Nurse responds, "Yes, sir, I'm sure you do; that's wonderful." She explains that maintaining the spark of love in a relationship contributes to marital well-being and to one's general mental and physical health.

Sam speaks. He says that Susan is a good woman, as good now as when he met her sixty nine years ago. Ms. Nurse, responds, "That's wonderful; you have a very good view of your wife." She explains that having a high estimation of one's spouse makes problem solving much easier and brings general satisfaction with life.

Sam speaks. He says that he and Susan really enjoy each other, after all these years, and that they always look for the good in each other. Ms. Nurse responds, "I'm so glad to hear that." She explains that couples should find ways to enjoy each other, instead of allowing a marital relationship to become stale, adding that maturity calls for adults to carry their responsibility for themselves in every relationship, including marriage.

PART FOUR: GRIEVING AND BEYOND

Sam speaks. "Do you hear what I'm saying?" Ms. Nurse says that she believes she hears what Mr. Purveys is saying.

"What is that?" Sam asks. Squirming a little, Ms. Nurse states that she heard Mr. Purveys say that he loves his wife, that she is a good woman, and that they really enjoy being together. She explains that professional health care providers are trained to listen well. She explains that her training for listening well takes several forms, including numerous group projects that require careful listening and just as many conversations with supervisory nurses, over a period of several years.

Sam speaks, slowly, reflectively, kindly, and embraces Ms. Nurse with his words, as if to nurture her to health. "Everything good that I know is what I learned because I know her. She is my comfort. She is my joy. She makes me what I am as a man. I've never questioned whether I should believe what she says. Now, I wonder, of course, whether I have heard the last words she will ever say. I don't know. But, you know, even if I had to lay down my life for hers, I would be honored to do so. It looks like I can't lay down my life for hers because she will go first. But I do know that if every minute I've got until then will be used to make her as comfortable as she can be. I am so proud to know her. Even in her illness, she has let me know that I am loved, and that I am important to her. And I do the same for her. When we were dating, I could not afford to entertain Susan. That didn't seem to matter to her. More often than not, we just walked, talked and held hands. We just about wore out the road in front of her house. I was slow to ask her to marry me because I had so little to offer her, except for me, of course. She seemed to feel the same way about herself. After we married, though, we still couldn't afford much. So, we still walked a lot. And, you know, as we walked back then, we decided that we would always walk a lot together. And we have. We said that we would keep things simple. And we pretty much have done that, too. Even when we had two kids, we walked. We started to walk because we couldn't afford to do anything else. But the more we walked and the more we talked, the more we knew that no one else in the world knew us as well as we knew each other.

We stayed busy with other things, but we always walked. Except, of course, when Susan was late in her pregnancies and right after the kids were born. And I cut my leg real bad once in a car wreck. But otherwise, we walked. We were involved with kids and school and a lot of community activities, but we walked. I believe that she understood me as well as I understood myself and I understood her as well as she understood herself. It has always been enjoyable just knowing her. And we never followed a script. We just talked. We let ourselves go with each other. We learned to be honest, to let it all show. And we found such joy in that. We know that we could buy groceries, without contaminating our decisions with unspoken questions or feelings. We could play with the kids, without making it a contest between us. We could manage our money, without fear that the other one may have secret uses for it. We could decorate the house, without suspecting that the other one might be getting his way. We were truly free. We found that life is not about explaining. It is about walking and talking, loving and letting yourself be loved. It's simple, if you let it be."

Sam stopped. He surveyed the face of the nurse, as if to wonder whether she had heard what he said, whether she had allowed herself to be simple and unexplained.

Sam spoke, again, "I fight against letting it be simple. But it is. When you come to our home to care for us, you have a job to do. I know that and understand it. Whether you enjoy it or not, you still have a job to do. It must be difficult to let your guard down, when you go to homes and see death about to happen. I understand it if you want to keep your guard up. That's okay. I would never want to change what you need to do for yourself. I do want to invite you into our home, though, as if you are as welcome as any one who could come here. I want to invite you to come into our lives and to experience with us this new intimacy, this walk together until Susan dies. We still walk: it's just that now we do everything but move our feet. It's still our walk together, though. And I'm asking you to join us.

Would you let us know you? Would you let yourself be known? Would you talk with Susan, just like she was your most intimate friend? Would you listen to her with the heart of a sister? You see, there aren't many ways that Susan is going to find comfort these days. Would you let her have the comfort of a friend, by being a friend with her? We prefer to have a friend and not a stranger caring for her while she is at her worst, less able than ever before to take care of herself."

Sam felt the impending loss of his life-long friend, as he spoke. He choked. His lip curled, with the tension of uncontrolled emotion. He spoke in a voice that told everything, even as his words were close to anguished silence. He stopped. His tears flowed.

Sam slumped, maybe with the knowledge that he would not lift his shoulders, again. In a tired body, he tried to do the good thing. He told his nurse that life is worthwhile, even in the face of death. In this moment, though, he had exhausted himself. In exposing his life-long devotion to Susan, he exposed his impending loss. He searched the room through the blurred vision of tear-filled eyes. He could not turn his eyes in any direction that would conceal his pain.

His nurse moved to him, sat beside him, and held him. She cried. There was nothing to explain.

The Eternal Now

I wait. And I wait some more. This is not what I do well. But I wait. I expect the call to come any minute. It is an important call, you know. You don't seem to be as concerned as I am. But this call could tell me whether I live or I die some time soon. I can't concentrate on anything else. How could I?

What could compare with the question of whether I live or die? And it all comes down to a phone call. It seems crazy, but it's real.

This is really happening to me. I try to tell myself that it's not real, that it will just go away, if I just go on with everything that I am supposed to be doing. But all I can do right now is wait.

No work. No television. No reading. No nothing. Nothing. Not a darn thing. I don't know whether to be afraid or to celebrate, to plan for the end or scream with joy because I can begin again. I just don't know. What do you do when you just don't know? I don't know. So, I wait.

Am I going live or die? I just don't know. You know what I think about, though? I think about times I have failed and felt like a fool and how important those times seemed to be at the time, but how little difference they made. Of course, I failed and felt like a fool. That's what human beings do.

But I think more about how much I have to do. How many summer days I have to walk in the grass and maybe how limited they are. How many special moments I might want to hug my kids that I won't have anymore. How many gifts I would like to give, especially to people who need something from me—you know, some food, maybe clothes, maybe some money. I'm talking about whatever it takes to make life better for someone for whom I can make a difference, a real difference.

But for now I wait. And I wonder what things might be life when I am gone. I don't know. The idea of death cuts pretty deep right now. I have to think about how I can take advantage of whatever life I have left. I don't know. I don't know what to think.

PART FOUR: GRIEVING AND BEYOND

When the phone rings, I hope I can answer it. I don't want to. I can't avoid it, but I don't want to know what the answer is. We'll see.

I wait. Dr. Coles said that she would call at four thirty. It's getting close to four thirty, now. I could have gone to her office after she got the results from the lab, but I would have had to wait until tomorrow. So, I asked her to call me today. She promised me she would. So, here I am, waiting.

If I had wings, I'd fly out of here right now. I would just enjoy the freedom of flying around and going anywhere I wanted to go. But I know I'm stuck here. I feel like my insides are flying, but I'm not going anywhere. I'm just here waiting. It's hard to do that.

With so little of life left, I want to sip every drop of it slowly and let every minute of it—good and bad—fill me beyond my capacity to hold it or to imagine it. I guess that's the way you thing when you realize how precious life is.

Look at me. I sigh so heavily I might blow you away. But I have to face the truth. And, no matter what it is, I have to consider what I do with the rest of my life. What kind of life do I want it to be? I guess the answer is that, no matter what I hear, I want to discover ways of b being good, of doing good. I'm not very clear about exactly I should do, but I do know that I will do what is right. It is a matter of acting in ways that match my conscience, what I feel is most strongly about inside. It is a matter of setting aside what others might think and doing what is right. I have always wanted to do what is right and to appreciate every precious moment of life, but a lot of things have gotten in the way. You know, work, money, bills, trying to make things better for me and my family. But, when it comes right down to a matter of life and death, we have to place our weight on life, and try to do everything we can to make life better. That's what I'm saying. I feel like I must do everything I can to make life better. Not just as a big idea that sounds good, but by doing all I can for as many people as I can. Life must be treated as a precious thing. You know. Does this make sense to you?

THE ETERNAL NOW

When you are waiting for a phone call that tells you, "You are going to die," you think a lot more about life. Of course, I have to think about the fact that I may not have much life...

R...I...N...G!

My heart began to pound! I could feel it.

R...I...N...G!

Oh, God, what do I do now?

R...I...N...G!

Hello.

Hi, this is Doctor Coles. I just got a fax from the lab. For once, they got it to me on time. And I just wanted to go over some of it with you, if you have a minute. Actually, there's not much to go over. I'd be glad to ago over any of the details you want, but essentially, all the screens are negative. There's none of the things we expected. None of the things we prepared you for were there. So, basically, you're okay. I hope we didn't get you too stirred up, for nothing. Blah, blah, blah, blah, blah.

I don't know what to think. I have to take time to absorb this.

I'm okay. Life has begun again. Now, what do I do? I have a new start. And I don't know what to do with it. I guess I have more life that I thought I would. For one thing, I guess I'll go to work tomorrow. But I'm not sure what to do with all the life I've got, now that I know I've got it. So, for now, I'll just wait.

More Than I Could Hope For

Is today the day I die? I'm not sure. I do know that the illness that has accompanied me for the past four years has become such a part of my life that I cannot live without it. Of course, I would like to live without it, but I won't. It will kill me. Thus, I ask myself whether I may do myself and others a favor by killing myself. If I kill myself, I can at least manage the timing of my death, instead of allowing my illness to steal the functioning parts of my body until I have no control over any aspect of my body—eating moving, even smiling, eliminating, and maybe, most important, thinking. The picture of me as one whose body goes silently and emotionless from one day to the next, with no control over what is done to me, causes me to feel quite sad.

I look at my husband. His furrowed face shows such deep concern. As much as he tries to play the hero for me, doing everything he can to make me comfortable, his eyes show a lot of hurt and his slumped shoulders show defeat. Still, he smiles, as if his smiling may become such a habit that he will be happy because he can't stop smiling.

The night is particularly difficult. As the black of night surrounds the house, I feel like death may be speaking to me in a louder and louder voice each night. And when we turn off the lights, I choke on the terror, the alarm of a million gunshots aimed at my heart. The bullets never hit me, though, but the terror does. The dark and the terror close in. Is this my last night? Did I just get the last glimpse of my mother's picture? Did I feel the cold and beautiful tile on the bathroom floor for the last time? If I close my eyes, will I ever see our nicely carved headboard wall again? Can I trace the seams of the quilt on the bed with my fingers enough to convince myself that I'm not dead yet? Have I spoken my last word? Sometimes, I can't help but speak out loud, just to know that I am still alive. Have I seen my kids for the last time? I hate that question, but life is all questions for me. There are no answers when your life is quite possibly only one breath longer.

MORE THAN I COULD HOPE FOR

Yes, I ponder death. I really have little else to think about. I brood about what death might mean to me and my family.

I try to give thanks for all of my life, so far. For flipping an umbrella under my older sister's skirt and exposing her panties in a crowd of other kids. For making my mother a ceramic sculpture for Mother's Day. We never could tell what it was. For my grandmother, my other mother, who seemed to provide an anchor for me when I was adrift. For the big tree next to the driveway that we climbed and to which we tied our swings. For falling in love and getting married. For making pictures with my dad on the turnaround with sidewalk chalk. For kisses, with all the special people in my life. For singing "Darling, You Can Count on Me" with my cousin. For family debates while we ate dinner. For sweet secrets kept, between me and my husband, between me and my Mom, between me and my son, between me and. . . .

I really am thankful for many things, but every attempt to give attention to these things slides into terror as I recognize that I want to feel thankful for them because I am near the time when I will lose them forever. So, instead of giving attention to gratitude and allowing terror to overcome me, I try to be neutral. I try to be as mindless as I can be, but I am not good at being mindless. I need to think about things, to be curious, figure out what is happening, to know what everyone else who is important to me is doing. I want to claim some small measures of being normal.

For now, listening to my music is okay. But more important, listening to your voice and feeling your hand on mine are more than I could ever hope for.

Feeling your hand on mine—touching me—is more than I could hope for.

I don't feel the terror, now. I am ready to rest, now. Thank you.

You are more than I could hope for. Feeling your hand on mine is more than I could hope for.

The Last Word

And, finally . . . *This Moment,* below, was written as a tribute to a nurse who cared for terminally ill patients. At least, it is a reminder of what is important about living and loving.

The Moment

The bounty of days—

so many fresh tomatoes to enjoy, so much ice cream, so many silly antics from the kids.

The sun comes and goes. My days are endless.

Little could little be better than it is.

But as I see my patients, my tears sometimes roll, like the rain on the window.

Their time lacks the endless quality that I assume is there for me.

Their pain sounds the alarm on their life's clock, as surely as the alarm on my clock wakes me each morning. A life is about to end.

Their last moment softly ticks away. Their time expires.

The time of their special and loved ones stops, too, as they feel anguish more than comfort, loss more than hope, death more than life. This is their moment.

And I hold them, wishing for the energy of the sun, wanting and willing for all my love and hope to penetrate their souls so that their moment is less painful, less overwhelming.

And, then, I think of home and you.

And I think of precious life, so teeming with possibility and so temporary, and how I might define myself without you, without home and your presence.

And, when I get home, I am pleased when you hold me, refusing to wonder why this embrace is so long and why my tears come so readily.

You know that this embrace could be our last, but you don't know.

Is this the one, the last tender moment?

And this kiss? And this "I love you?" And this intimate look?

This is the moment. It is God's moment.

The Last Last Word

The Last, Last Word: May each of your moments fill you with recognizing and feeling the wonderful presence of those who love you, including God.

Bibliography

"2017 Hurricane Harvey: Facts, FAQs, and how to help." World Vision, accessed October 24, 2019, https://www.worldvision.org/disaster-relief-news-stories/2017-hurricane-harvey-facts.

Centers for Disease Control and Prevention. "National Center for Health Statistics, Deaths and Mortality," CDC.gov. http://www.cdc.gov/nchs/fastats/deaths.htm (Accessed January 29, 2019).

Child Welfare Information Gateway. (2019). *Foster care statistics 2017.* Washington, DC: U.S. Department of Health and Human Services, Children's Bureau, 2017.

"College Grief & Actively Moving Forward (AMF)." What's Your Grief, accessed October 24, 2019, https://whatsyourgrief.com/college-grief/.

"Death and Mortality." Centers for Disease Control and Prevention, accessed October 24, 2019, from: https://www.cdc.gov/nchs/fastats/deaths.htm.

Doka, Ken. "What Is Grief?" Hospice Foundation of America, accessed October 25, 2019, https://hospicefoundation.org/Grief-(1)/What-to-Expect.

"FBI Releases 2018 Crime Statistics." Federal Bureau of Investigation—U.S. Department of Justice, accessed October 24, 2019, https://www.fbi.gov/news/pressrel/press-releases/fbi-releases-2018-crime-statistics.

"Grief Speaks." Grief Speaks, accessed October 24, 2019, http://www.griefspeaks.com/id113.html.

"List of U.S. states by homicide rate." Wikipedia, accessed October 24, 2019, https://en.wikipedia.org/wiki/List_of_U.S._states_by_homicide_rate.

"Marital status of the U.S. population, by sex 2018." Statista, accessed October 24, 2019, https://www.statista.com/statistics/242030/marital-status-of-the-us-population-by-sex/.

Martin, Francis A., *Full Life: A Workbook for Spiritual Recovery from Addictions.* Nashville, Tennessee: Green Hills Press, 2010.

"Miscarriage Statistics." Hopexchange, accessed October 24, 2019, http://www.hopexchange.com/Statistics.htm.

"Infertility." Centers for Disease Control and Prevention, accessed October 24, 2019, https://www.cdc.gov/nchs/fastats/infertility.htm.

"Murder map: Deadliest U.S. cities." CBS News, accessed October 24, 2019, https://www.cbsnews.com/pictures/murder-map-deadliest-u-s-cities.

New International Version. All Scripture quotations, unless otherwise indicated, are taken from the Holy Bible, New International Version®, NIV®. Copyright ©1973, 1978, 1984, 2011 by Biblica, Inc.™ Used by permission of Zondervan. All rights reserved .worldwide. www.zondervan.com The "NIV" and "New International Version" are trademarks registered in the United States Patent and Trademark Office by Biblica, Inc.™

"Preventing Suicide in the United States." Centers for Disease Control and Prevention, accessed on October 24, 2019, from: https://www.cdc.gov/violenceprevention/pdf/RO1-FactsheetSuicidePrevention-508.pdf.

BIBLIOGRAPHY

Rando, Therese. A. How to Go on Living When Someone You Love Dies. New York, New York: Bantam Edition (1991).

Social Security Administration. "Annual Statistical Report on the Social Security Disability Insurance Program, 2018." Washington, DC: Social Security Administration, 2019, p. 11.

TransAmerica Center for Retirement Studies. "A Precarious Existence: How Today's Retirees Are Financially Faring in Retirement, December 2018." Los Angles, CA: TransAmerica Center for Retirement Studies, 2019, p. 11.

Untitled. Centers for Disease Control and Prevention, accessed October 24, 2019, from: http://www.cdc.gov/nchs/data/misc/atlasres.pdf.

www.ingramcontent.com/pod-product-compliance
Lightning Source LLC
Chambersburg PA
CBHW051926160426
43198CB00012B/2063